Living the Leadership Choice

Living the Leadership Choice

A Guide to Changing Your Life
and the World

KATHLEEN SCHAFER

iUniverse, Inc.
Bloomington

Living the Leadership Choice
A Guide to Changing Your Life and the World

iUniverse books may be ordered through booksellers or by contacting:

iUniverse
1663 Liberty Drive
Bloomington, IN 47403
www.iuniverse.com
1-800-Authors (1-800-288-4677)

ISBN: 978-1-4620-3449-9 (sc)
ISBN: 978-1-4620-3451-2 (hc)
ISBN: 978-1-4620-3450-5 (ebk)

Printed in the United States of America

iUniverse rev. date: 11/29/2011

Contents

Part III

Dedicated to my sons, Nick and Jake,
whose passion to see the world as it can be rather than as it is fuels my desire
to help people create meaningful change in their lives.
For their inspiration and love, I am grateful.

Preface

The Journey of Self-Discovery

From my earliest childhood memories, I had a burning desire to be the first woman president of the United States. The competitive side of me loved the idea of being the first to do something, and the compassionate, creative part of me wanted to solve real-world problems. Even as a child, I couldn't understand why slums existed, how people could ignore our environment, and why so many of my peers lived impoverished lives—not just economically, but socially, emotionally, and educationally as well. The truth be told, I too was living an impoverished life, but it seemed far easier to focus on everyone else's problems than it did to deal with my own.

So despite growing up in an incredibly dysfunctional and abusive household, I resolved to single-handedly save the world. I felt that if I could contain all the madness going on in my personal life, I could build an external image of success using all the wonderful qualities I could bring to addressing world's problems. Starting in grade school, I put everything I could into being the best I could possibly be. I diligently applied myself to my studies, even in the areas I detested, engaged in sports, was involved in student government, community service, and with what little time I had left did a bit of socializing and tried to have fun.

During my junior year in high school, my history teacher came to me and suggested that I intern at the state capitol for our local Representative. Then-state Representative Debbie Stabenow agreed to allow me to work in her office. What a wonderful opportunity to learn from a woman who was doing exactly what I wanted to do! She was a part of the first wave of women to run for public office, and today she is Michigan's junior senator. The opportunity to work for her changed the course of my life in many ways. By the time I graduated from high school, not only had I worked at the state capitol for nearly one year, I had been elected as a director for an international service organization, elected senior class president, was team captain in volleyball and softball, voted most likely to succeed by my classmates, and started, ran, and organized a host of other activities and events. What an auspicious start to a great life—or was it?

Having been introduced to the world of politics I chose to stay in Lansing, Michigan, and attend James Madison College at Michigan State University. Of course, given my burning desire to save the world, I worked thirty hours per week for Representative Stabenow and subsequently for the departments of commerce, transportation and management, and budget, all while graduating from college within three years.

While working in Michigan's state government during this time, I met the man who would become my husband for seventeen years and the father of my two sons. Shortly after I graduated and got married, the governor for whose administration I had been working lost the election. This change ushered in another important opportunity, which was to leave government service and support effective leadership from the community.

Having seen how government worked up close, I was dismayed by how most elected officials operated. Rare were the conversations about creating truly effective policies and frequent were the discussions about power, position, and electoral success. I was shocked to find that the path I had wanted to pursue was so distasteful to me, and with my usual vigor I set about to solve the problem. The idea of creating a program in Michigan modeled after one in North Carolina that trained people to not only run for office but also how to lead when they got there was intriguing.

During the next few years, I helped to establish and run the Michigan Political Leadership Program at Michigan State University. (The MPLP continues its mission and has graduated many of Michigan's current political leaders.) I started a consulting firm that was sold to Michigan's largest for-profit think tank, and five years later decided that I wanted to work directly with those running for public office, particularly women and other underrepresented groups, as I strongly believed that we would never be able to create effective public policies until everyone had a voice at the table.

In 1995, I started Leadership Connection with the help and support of my mentor Cathy Allen. At the time, I had no idea how powerful the business's name would become in my life's work, and it is one of the wonderful synchronicities I have come to appreciate in my life. During the following few years, I traveled hundreds of thousands of miles speaking at events, working on campaigns, hosting a nationally syndicated radio show, and, beginning in 1996, teaching at The Graduate School of Political Management at The George Washington University. Again, a purely unanticipated invitation by the school's dean, Chris Arterton, ushered in another wonderful opportunity to explore leadership through the classroom experience and develop my ideas on what it takes to create change in our world.

In 1997, my world shifted in an entirely new way when I became a mother to my incredible son. His amazing younger brother followed five years later. While I continued to work part-time, my beautiful feminine qualities emerged for the first time in my life. As a women in the rough and tumble worlds of politics, business, and the media, I could hang with the toughest of them. After becoming a mother, my desire for the thrill of competition simply for the sake of the game waned as I became much more conscious of the life-affirming qualities essential in effective leadership. I was stunned by the connection I felt to every other human being on the planet—every one of us had been *born* and was carried by another human who brought us into the world. Living this sacred experience with my own children tied me to all others and helped me to see the senselessness of competing with others who desired the same basic things—peace, love, joy, and happiness.

Given what was going on with me as a mother, it was no surprise that my professional work shifted as well. I no longer wished to engage in playing the game—I longed to transform it. As a result, I began working with clients to help them identify their unique qualities and how they could bring them into the world. My coaching, teaching, and speaking moved in new directions as I plunged into learning new theories and ways of living a whole and balanced life. Through these experiences I began to appreciate my talents in new ways and to fully understand that part of my purpose was to distill and encapsulate a wide variety of knowledge in ways that people could practically apply in their lives.

The final major shift that occurred for me prior to writing this book was the decision to end my marriage. After years in pursuit of the American dream, we had finally made it big: a beautiful house in a highly sought-after neighborhood, the kids in a fabulous private school, a sailboat, great vacations, and all the "things" money could buy. The realization that money doesn't buy happiness is always more jarring when it happens to you. Having finally achieved the accoutrements of success after years toiling on work without time for quality relationships, creativity, and joy in daily life the affluent life was shockingly shallow—the quality of the surroundings may have changed, although the quality of life had not. The realization that it doesn't matter how much you have if you aren't fulfilled and happy inside was a bitter pill to swallow, and I knew that I didn't want to live without true happiness any longer. That decision was the first step on a path that, while extremely difficult at times, has led to ever-increasing joy and happiness in my life.

That is what this book is about—the journey of life. It is a journey that is rarely discussed in contemporary times because it is far easier to focus on the external world than it is to deal with what is going on inside of us. For the majority of my life I tried to fix things in my life by working on outside problems while all the remedies I was seeking could only be found by exploring who I truly am. That is why the focus of my life and work is no longer about external accomplishments that lead to happiness. It is about how to build a life based on the extraordinary person each of us already is and then to create and allow our dreams to manifest in beautiful and unexpected ways. While the idea of this sounds good to most people, the difficulty is in knowing what to do each day to ground these practices in our daily lives. That is where my talent lies—in guiding others through the process of letting go of the story we have been told about what will make us happy and supporting them in listening to their innate wisdom, which already knows how to live it. This is not a skill I have mastered, nor do I ever expect to; rather, it is a journey that I am committed to walking with full awareness every day of my life. If I can offer guidance to others as they walk the same path, then the journey will be enriched for everyone.

The essence of what I have learned throughout my life and during my twenty-plus years as a professional is in this book. Integrating leadership, business, management, organizational development, physiology, time management, education, health, communication, nutrition, Ayurveda, and a variety of other disciplines, I have developed a twenty-eight-day course that comprises the bulk of this book. I love to learn new ideas and reflect on how they support the process of self-understanding, for *you* are the foundation of everything in your life. Each of us desires to create beautiful things in our lives, and it can only happen if we are secure in our love for who we are.

I am not sharing my story to set myself apart for my unrelenting pursuit of external success. In fact in some respects, I have failed to accomplish as much I would have liked. I share my story to show that I am just like you. Regardless of what your life has looked like to this point, I am certain that you have believed that happiness only comes through external accomplishments. The human experience is one we share together—we are more alike than different. When each person embraces the unique qualities he or she brings to the world and fully lives them, then we will create a society filled with much greater personal satisfaction and success because we need fully engaged citizens to make our world work. As you read through the first part of this book, you will come to understand how I have (re)defined leadership, and hopefully you will begin to see yourself as the leader that you already are. Thank you for the opportunity to be a part of your journey, just as you have now become a part of mine.

Introduction

True Happiness and Success Start with You

Leading Ourselves, Changing Our World

Everything in the world is changing. We see it and sense it every day. For those approaching middle age, we hearken back to our childhoods that seem somehow strangely passive and full of naivety. School days were filled with moderate degrees of learning, and the worst things that happened were playground tussles or the easily forgotten minor embarrassments of childhood. Summers stretched endlessly, and play consisted of finding the neighbors and going off for a day of exploration. Routines were relegated to classrooms, and homes ran at an easier pace. While the cold war loomed large, the energy crisis and Iranian hostage situation were the biggest international crises with which we had to contend.

The experience of our children today is much different. For many, the reality that "bad people" can fly planes into buildings, that guns can and often do come to school, that our planet is warming up, that intractable wars in the Middle East kill not only soldiers but civilians with abandon, and that Mom and Dad are working more and playing less are the defining experiences in childhood. They are everyday realities with which we must contend. As adults, we experience these same world pressures along with the new reality that we need two incomes to keep our families afloat and the pressure to ensure that our children are well-rounded through an endless series of sports, music, and academic activities. There is little time left to sleep in a day, let alone pursue activities that are enjoyable and nurturing for us.

The solutions to these challenges appear elusive. What can I do to achieve world peace? How can I stop global warming? Should I be the one to step away from supporting my children's frenetic pace only to have them end up as life's losers? And if I hold it together, somewhere in the future will there be five minutes for me to take some time for myself? In the face of seemingly insurmountable problems, we translate all of these issues into modern life's favorite buzzword—stress.

Everyone has it, many in extreme doses. In fact, a growing number of people have so much of it that it becomes their new reality. It is the seductive companion that keeps us feeling a part of the group. Ask anyone how they are doing and almost without a doubt the answer will be "busy," or "okay, just lots going on." How did we get here, and is it a coincidence that as the craziness in our lives escalates, so too does the chaos in the world?

The idea that "the answer is simple, it is the doing that is the hard part," holds true for a reason. Don't we understand what would make our lives better? A survey by *USA Today* and Gallop in December 2010 found that this generation is less satisfied with their leisure time than their parents were, dropping from 76 percent in 1963 to less than 66 percent currently. People may feel they have enough free time today, but most of them rush through it instead of taking the time to connect with those whom they are sharing their free time with. It is no mystery that people want to slow down, appreciate life, and stop feeling that they are constantly on the move—so why don't we do it? Recently, a friend who leads a particularly chaotic life that is further complicated by her family's unending battles with a host of sicknesses (caused by stress) remarked how wonderful it was for her to spend some time on a beach alone with her husband. "I had forgotten what life was supposed to be like!" she declared.

In this same way, don't we all know what is causing the sickness in the world? Do we really believe that by waging war we are going to stop terrorism? Is destroying a country going to lead to peace among its citizens? Is the harm done to our men and women in arms going to stop the minute they return from the battlefield? We know the answers to these questions, yet it is this knowing that keeps us from pursing the solutions that will truly make a difference. Why? Because if we pursue the course that leads toward peace and contentment, it would require us to alter our thinking about how we live our lives. And who among us embraces the unknown, let alone pursues it?

We have all bought into an agreement about our lives. If we "live well" and "do the right things" such as go to school, get a good education, a good job, and raise a family, at some magical moment after all these accomplishments are complete we will be rewarded with the golden years. This fantasy includes visions of days spent on sandy beaches or in pursuit of lifelong ambitions shoved aside in the race through real life. Yet, at what cost are we selling our souls for the pursuit of this dream? We speed through our lives in an attempt to earn more, consume more, all to ensure that at some point there will be enough so that we can stop doing all the things we have been doing our entire adult lives. No wonder so many people are depressed in their retirement!

Further depressing is the emerging reality that the golden years of retirement rarely result in the elusive search for happiness. In fact, more studies are showing a precipitous decline in people's health once they retire and live a life of non-engagement and commitment to the world. These studies also show that despite a lifetime of work and service to family and community, there are often not enough resources available to create the lives people desire, and impoverishment takes hold literally and figuratively. So where does this leave us? Doomed to a life filled with responsibilities within a world that grows more menacing by the day? Can we change the pace of our lives, let alone world events?

The answer is yes. The first step is to recognize the control we have to create change. Gandhi's wise words, "Be the change you wish to create in the world" can be interpreted on many levels and at each we can find the path to peace in our lives and in our world. How many of us have looked at situations in our families, communities, and even our country and said, "What a mess"? We become angry, resentful, annoyed, and bothered by the actions of others, which ultimately leads to frustration over how stupid everyone else is behaving. We become consumed by our awareness of the mistakes of others. This leads to one of the first truths about creating peace in our lives—we will *never* be able to change anyone else; the only person we have any power to change is ourselves.

Just releasing ourselves from the stress of figuring out how to solve everyone else's bad behavior is relaxing. You may believe the president made a huge mistake in going to war, yet there is nothing you can do to change his actions and beliefs. Many would argue that by protesting the war, we could change his mind and make him see the error of his ways. There are two misnomers in this argument. One is that by "fighting," that person is engaged in the same type of behavior he is protesting, just at a different level (in other words, you are waging war with words, marches, blogs, and so forth, which are justified by your belief in the cause). The second misnomer is that *no one* can change another person's mind—each person must decide for himself or herself how he or she wants to engage with the world. Everyone has to take responsibility for their actions, and if a president or leader decides to change his politics or policies, it is not going to be because of a peace march, failed election, or public pressure. It is going to be because he has decided to do something different.

So what can one person *do*? We are a society that believes in action; action denotes that we are alive and engaged. Yet the first word of Gandhi's quote is "be." This concept is difficult for many people. What do you mean, "be"? Be what? Be whom? By when? Embodied in the idea of being is the concept of allowing ourselves to be comfortable in the moment, in the here and now. What is happening right now? Realize that in this moment everything is okay, you have control over what you are experiencing. You are not under the influence of a government, a boss, a teacher, or even your child—*you* are in control. You have absolute freedom to choose how you experience this moment based on the unique qualities that make you who you are. This leads us to the next part of the quote: "the change."

What change would you like to experience in your life? Would you like to have more satisfaction with your job? Do you desire less stress? More time? More quiet moments? World peace? What can you do to create these things in your life? What can you change to bring this shift about? If you are a less stressed person who is fulfilled in your work and thus more peaceful—will that have an impact on the world? What do you think happens when you have a bad day and find yourself huffing and puffing while waiting in line at the supermarket? Do other people around you pick up on your anxiety? How do you think the cashier feels after you've tongue-lashed her for having to wait while she finds a price? Does she go home, taking with her your stress and bad mood, and yell at her kids because she's had a bad day?

What do you communicate to your own children when you walk through the door? What few people realize is that bad moods, anxieties, and anger don't go away once you have dumped them on others. They just keep getting passed around from person to person. So though you may have snapped at only three people after your bad day, like a pebble tossed into a pond, your anger has a ripple effect that could affect hundreds of people by the end of the evening. Perhaps you really can change world.

On the flip side, you have the power to stop all the bad attitudes that are passed on to you throughout the day. So your boss was upset because an important client canceled a meeting and yelled at you to get it rescheduled. Do you have to take on his fears and anxieties? By keeping your attention in the moment, you are able to stop his negative energy from penetrating you—you can discard the negativity in favor of your peace of mind. Do you think you can create a change by calmly calling the client and learning that there had been a sudden death in her family and she would be happy to reschedule next week? Or perhaps she simply had a project deadline and didn't have time for the meeting today. Would you have helped her by not bringing additional anxiety to the conversation through your approach? Would you be able to easily meet her needs and communicate your success to your boss? Wouldn't everyone feel better as a result of these kinds of exchanges? Now you have created a more peaceful day—exactly what you have intended for yourself—along with the wonderful side benefit of easing the day of everyone around you. Now you are responsible for moving peace through the world, not anger.

Another way to look at this phenomenon is through the prism of the Virginia Tech shooting. We can take an important leadership lesson from the senseless loss of thirty-two lives in one of the worst shootings in American history. Lives both young and old, so full of promise, were cut short by one individual whose personal story was clearly full of pain, anger, and despair. How else could someone do such a thing? While situations such as these can never be fully explained nor even conceived of by the vast majority of us, what responsibility do we all have for creating a culture that allows this toxic mix of circumstances to exist?

Reaction from countries and their leaders throughout the world provides a wonderful mirror for American self-examination, but we rarely use it because too many of us prefer to engage in one of our favorite pastimes—looking for someone to blame. Of course, it is so much easier to find fault with campus officials or the police department for not alerting students sooner, or parents and professors for not getting this young man help. Yet we need to ask ourselves what responsibility we bear as a society that condones "hands-off" policies that prevent us from helping those who may need it most? Why do we too often succumb to the convenience of turning a blind eye to challenging situations for which we don't have a simple solution?

More importantly, will we engage in the self-examination of a national culture of violence, as was so aptly pointed out by Pierre Chiquet, a seventy-seven-year-old retired French aerospace engineer who said, "Violence is more imbued in American society than in ours. The most dramatic aspect is that they even transport their violence to the rest of the world" (*Washington Post*, April 18, 2007). What do we expect to happen in our country when we began a war that has unleashed this level of destruction every day? This thought was not lost on Ranya Riyad, a nineteen-year-old college student in Baghdad who said, "It is a little incident if we compare it with the disasters that have happened in Iraq. We are dying every day" (Ibid). We will never stop this type of violence in the United States until we stop perpetuating it elsewhere and in our everyday lives through mass media and entertainment. We are not separate—we all live on this planet together, and the energy of violence cannot be stopped; it can only be replaced by leaders who are willing to create a society that values every individual and his or her quality of life.

So as we look for lessons and for hope out of a senseless tragedy, let us look into our own lives and our own potential to change. Are we creating peace in our lives? Do we watch violent films or play violent video games for "entertainment"? Are we engaged in activities that harm other individuals, whether it is in business, on the playing field, or even in our social circles? People don't seem bothered by snide comments or attitudes that perpetuate separation as long as they are on the "in," but what happens to the child who grows up feeling like an outsider to our culture, groups, and communities? If we don't address the bullies and bad attitudes in our neighborhoods, how can we possibly expect peace will exist in the world?

This book is about the journey we must all make toward a peaceful, powerful, and effective existence for ourselves, our families, communities, and country. There is no other way to address the issues that face us personally, professionally, and societally. No longer can we think that a war-torn region in a faraway country won't affect us at home—we can't wage war in one land and not have it come home to roost in ours. We can't hide in the glass house of prosperity we have built upon individual freedom. It is time that we use this freedom not for our own gluttonous indulgences, but as a means by which to give the best of ourselves to our communities and our world. If we are to survive as a nation, and indeed a species, we must stop the narcissistic practices in our own lives and look toward the true rewards that come when one genuinely shares one's unique gifts with others.

We all know that money doesn't buy happiness, yet nearly every action we take is rooted in the pursuit of material comforts. Let us begin to think not about "what this means for me," but rather "what this means for us." As we begin to view our actions through a prism of collective experiences and solutions, we will make progress toward the goals that really matter to most individuals—happiness, peace, and joy in our lives and in the lives of others. As you read this book, keep Gandhi's quote at the forefront of your mind and think about the change *you* wish to create in the world.

Part I

What We Have and What We Want

Chapter 1

A New Definition of Effective Leadership

The textbook definition of leadership is "the action of leading a group or organization," and inherent in this description is the idea of one person standing above others, telling them what to do. This book is based on a wholly different concept of what leadership is about. My definition of leadership is "love in action." First love for self, then love for others, and finally acting each day in a way that honors the love you have for all. This is not a kumbaya experience where we forget the reality of what it is to live in the world; quite the opposite, it is about having the courage to live an open, honest life of connection to self and others that enhances our world rather than destroys it. If anyone doubts the courage needed to live love through action, try doing it for just one day. I promise you will never think it wimpy again.

Each one of us possesses talents, skills, and abilities that, combined with our passion for change, make us unique. The thrill of discovering what you uniquely have to offer the world allows you to open up greater happiness and make a meaningful contribution to your community. As you gain clarity about your talents and skills and articulate them to others, you attract support from people because they can see your vision and choose to be a part of it. This in turn gives them the opportunity to contribute their talents and skills, as change becomes a reality when complimentary skills sets come together to achieve a goal.

You begin this process by opening your eyes to the leader you already are—he or she is in there, perhaps more obscure than you would like, but there nonetheless. This book asks you to answer questions that will reveal the power you already have instead of looking for an external solution to change your life or the world around you.

I strongly recommend that you keep a written record of the exercises you do throughout the book; you may want to keep a journal or you may prefer Post-it notes—whatever feels best to you is fine. There are no right answers to these questions; in fact, your answers may change over time. What you should notice are the trends and threads that you will weave on your journey to becoming the leader you have always been.

Leadership: Where It All Begins

Where does leadership come from and how do we use it in our everyday lives? Everyone has ideas about who and what leaders are and whether they're born or they're made. Henry Kissinger said, "The mark of a great leader is to take his society from where it is to where it has never been.... Leaders must invoke an alchemy of great vision. Those leaders who do not are ultimately judged failures, even though they may be popular at the moment." Ultimately that's what leadership is about—first owning and understanding your inner energy and *then* putting your leadership skills into the world. It's about change. It's about working with people to create the changes that we want to see in our communities, in our organizations, in our governments, and in the world. Just importantly, as Kissinger alludes to, leadership is not about popularity in the moment; rather, it is about sustained contribution to real change that makes a positive difference in people's lives.

Leaders articulate a vision. They see where the possibility and promise exist, and they know how to effectively get people to move there. This requires a variety of skill sets in working with people—and it is not difficult. Most of the changes we want to create are in our immediate lives, and the key to success is becoming aware of our power and learning the recipe for walking people through the process.

Each of us has natural talents and abilities that we bring to the table, and our ability to identify them is important to the effectiveness of every leader. There are skills that we can learn and talents that can be developed as we progress as leaders throughout our lives; the seeds are already within us. By becoming aware of the journey that we are already on, we begin to understand that we are either dismissing our gifts and not using them in our daily lives or we are actively engaged in resisting what makes us tick and using our energies in service to others. Fully owning our talents, strengths, and skills and endeavoring each day to be and give our best is how we begin *Living the Leadership Choice.*

When you think about your leadership, first ask yourself, *Who are those leaders that I admire?* Begin to identify the leadership skills and talents that you see as valuable and important in the world. You will come to understand that these traits fall into the following four categories.

1. Seeing What Needs to Be Done

Leaders see what needs to be done. They know what can make a situation better, and often they are able to conceptualize a solution before people are even aware there is a problem. Leaders can see beyond the emotional reactions of different people, groups, and interests and are willing to move forward in a way that benefits everyone involved. For some people this means developing a grand plan, for others it may be the ability to see the next steps to be taken. In any case, a leader is one who not only sees a possible solution, but also is also willing to articulate it and take action.

One of my favorite leaders is Gandhi. He was able to envision freeing the people of India; he could see an India that would not always be a British colony. He was able to get beyond the reality of what was, to communicate that vision to others, and begin creating the change he wanted to see in the world. His vision and communication mobilized the forces and the people that were needed to create the change. It wasn't about him and what he could do alone—his leadership success came only after he was willing to stand up and communicate an idea of a better life and work with others to make it a reality. This quality in leaders is described as vision. Seeing what needs to be done requires us to develop this two-part skill: we must have a vision and we must be able to act on it and make it a reality.

There are many leaders who see beyond the horizon into our collective future. Become aware of those who are taking actions to change our world and observe how they are addressing their issues. As you observe leaders in your life, think about things that you want to change. This is an important element of leadership—focus on the changes that are in needed in your immediate life (i.e., the challenges you deal with every day). It is easy to put off leadership by thinking that you must wait until you can deal with the big issue when most problems are solved at the local level.

2. *Understanding the Underlying Forces at Play*

Effective leaders understand all the underlying forces that are at play. Leaders with a vision for change must also understand the factors that led to creating the current situation. What role did various people and groups play? What are the current attitudes of those who are impacted by the situation? What do they feel is the solution? What emotions are they experiencing as a result of the situation? Are *they* fully aware of all the underlying factors?

One example of where this wasn't considered is the Iraq War. A decision was made to invade Iraq as a response to what happened in the United States on 9/11 and to keep America safe from the use of weapons of mass destruction on our shores. But our government leaders weren't accurately looking at all of the underlying forces at play in America, Iraq, the Middle Eastern region, and the world. It turned out there were no weapons of mass destruction in Iraq. We now see that when we don't consider all of the underlying forces, we can't create the change we wish to see.

In reality, the United States is not creating a safer, more secure and freer society for Americans. In fact, in many ways we're doing exactly the opposite. More American lives have been lost in the war than were lost in the 9/11 attack. Thousands more American soldiers and their families are living with wounds and traumas suffered in the war. Tens of thousands Iraqi citizens have been killed and wounded, and their country and its infrastructure is in shambles—all the conditions that have proven to actually *drive* young men and women into terrorist activities. Former Vice President Dick Cheney's quote, ". . . because I really do believe that we will be greeted as liberators. The read we get on the people of Iraq is there

6

is no question but what they want to the get rid of Saddam Hussein and they will welcome as liberators the United States when we come to do that," shows that fundamentally, our nation's leaders did not understand the complex underlying factors of terrorism. America and the rest of the world will live with this mistake for generations.

Don't underestimate the power of understanding a situation as it relates to the change you wish to create. Leaders must make accurate assessments about a situation, who the players are, and what their agendas are, and most importantly, they must respect the views of everyone involved. Through genuine listening and understanding the concerns and needs of others, leaders demonstrate their respect and value for *everyone* involved in the process of change. Self-absorbed leadership never creates success. If you are not being honest and serving the interests of the whole, then lasting positive change is impossible.

3. *Courage to Take Action*

Courage is considered an essential quality of leadership. Often courage is viewed as the ability to be forceful, which is not accurate. True courage emanates from the challenge of doing something that scares us, of acting on behalf of the greater good without concern for personal gain and recognition. Courage is defined as "the spirit that enables a person to face difficulty, danger, pain, etc., without fear." It is also defined as "to act in accordance with one's beliefs, especially in spite of criticism." How often do we encounter people who come across as tough, yet when it comes to standing up for something they supposedly believe in, they seem unable to face those who disagree with them? Many people find it easier to go along with the crowd.

Courage is often considered a masculine characteristic—yet the reality is that true courage comes from the balance of both masculine and feminine principles. Before going further in this conversation on courage, it is important to make a few points on gender qualities as they relate to leadership:

- Masculine doesn't mean male, and feminine doesn't mean female. Indeed everyone has both masculine and feminine characteristics, and we need a balance of both to be effective leaders.

- The shorthand way to think about it is that masculine characteristics are those that pertain to strength, power, force, and action. Masculine qualities in the broadest sense are about what we need to survive, such as money, shelter, and food. Therefore, anyone who controls access to life essentials is working with masculine power. It is expressed in how one owns and wields power.

- The feminine characteristics in leadership are about the ability to give life and to create. Feminine leadership principles rely on the one's ability to gather resources to create something that did not exist before the process began.

- Despite what is often taught to us in Western culture, neither the masculine nor feminine is better or worse. Both are equally important *and* powerful. Both are essential to the success of all leaders.

The masculine and feminine components are important distinctions to understand because too often when people think about courage, they think of the masculine qualities that compel people to be tough, to wage war, and to control. This is a one-sided interpretation of courage; we need balance, and without feminine qualities like the creation of ideas greater than the sum of its parts, unabashed courage can create disastrous results. Once we understand the benefits of investing time, building consensus, and taking action at the *right* time, reverting to overzealous control and aggression looks like the outdated leadership tactics that they are.

Courage is having the strength to find a solution that meets everyone's needs rather than simply forcing others to go along with your idea of what is right. Anyone with enough money and power can force others to do what he or she wants. Only a courageous person is willing to invite others to share in the decision-making process and allow it to unfold on its own. That is the beautiful balance of masculine and feminine, and it is where true power lies.

Our society calls for courageous leadership today. One of the best examples is the 2008 Democratic presidential primary and the battle between Barack Obama and Hilary Clinton. One of the reasons the battle was so close is that the two candidates, a male and a female, exhibited a balance of these leadership characteristics. Hillary Clinton exemplifies many masculine leadership qualities. She accurately understands that our current political system rewards masculine leadership qualities. That mindset was revealed in her strategy to run as the inevitable nominee and to lead with powerhouse skills. Conversely, the male candidate, Barack Obama, embodied many feminine leadership qualities as he focused on consensus, bringing people together, and addressing problems in a bipartisan way. Americans want balanced leadership, and they were given the choice of the masculine embodied in the female and the feminine embodied in the male candidate.

The public understands that the old style of authoritarian leadership no longer works. In this race we observed two candidates espousing the opposite leadership styles in packages that brought out the balance in each of them—the female candidate was exhibiting more masculine characteristics and the male candidate embodied more feminine qualities. In the end we saw that as a nation, we are still more comfortable with a male leader who exhibits elements of feminine leadership power than we are with choosing a female who embodies strength and toughness.

Ironically, those qualities that the public was so attracted to during the election have proven not to serve President Obama as well in governing because he has failed to bring the necessary masculine qualities to the table to balance his other traits. Failure to powerfully articulate a vision and bring others along with him has kept many of his boldest and most necessary visions from becoming reality. At the same time, Secretary of State Clinton has relaxed and allowed more of her feminine qualities to rise in balance with her masculine qualities, thus becoming one of the most respected elected officials in the United States. This proves once again that what is initially perceived as a loss can become an unexpected victory.

Achieving balance between masculine and feminine leadership qualities may only require a subtle shift on your part, but when you do find that balance, you'll stand in the power of both and immediately understand the true potential of courageous leadership. The courage to do what's right without fear of rejection and to live the values you believe in will bring the greatest change to your life, your leadership, and your world.

4. *Leading from the Inside Out*

The leadership journey begins inside each one of us. If you don't know who you are and you're not grounded in your values, it is difficult to navigate life's challenges. What the outside world tells us is important is often contrary to the values that are essential to our personal happiness. If you don't take time to discover what you have to offer to others, to know your talents, strengths, and passions, it becomes difficult to effectively operate in the world. If your motivations and intentions are not clear, how are you going to effectively work with others?

What I call the "Rock Star" syndrome too often takes over people's lives. Frequently people ascend to positions of authority who want to be there simply because it's fun, exciting, and a huge ego boost. They have power, they get to be on television, they get to walk into a room and have people take notice, yet they have lost, or perhaps never had, the passion and purpose of serving others. Only by commitment to living our strengths and passion through service to others can we walk the path of leadership. You must lead from the inside out. Then when public accolades come, you are grounded in something other than ego and can successfully stand in the bright light of fame.

Effective leadership is not about the individual. It is not about one person succeeding or being elevated and emulated. It's about a leader serving in the way that he or she is most effective. On the journey to understanding leadership, think about yourself and think about leaders who have been effective. How they were able to stay grounded in who they are, in their values, and in their beliefs? Now consider how every single time we see a leader fall, it is because he or she has become disconnected from his or her truth. Never forget that true leaders are those who make real world change and live their passion.

A fantastic example of the power of leading from the inside out is Al Gore; he is a leader who lost his way but ultimately came back to it.

When he lost the 2000 presidential election, he wasn't using his voice and power. At the beginning of his campaign he was thought of as "Clinton light," then he morphed into the technological candidate, and then he became the environmental candidate. Throughout the campaign he never owned his unique leadership power, and the public knew that he was not connected to himself—an essential leadership quality.

Since losing the election and finding his voice, he has arguably accomplished more than he could have as president. Just a few short years after his devastating defeat, he was able to go to any city in the world to speak about global warming and command the attention of thousands of people because it was clear he was living his passion. If he were still in politics, or even as president, he would be hustling to get people to listen to him.

By working to stop global warming, Al Gore has lived his passion in a way that has allowed him to be the change that he wants to create. He put together a slide show and starting talking to whoever would listen to him. He did this with no personal agenda, but simply to get his message out. When you live your passion without regard for what *you* get from it, you reap much greater benefits. After all, do you really think he did all this so he could win an Academy Award and the Nobel Peace Prize? That's living your passion, that's living from the inside out. It wasn't about getting into a leadership position; it was about finding his passion and having the courage to act in an effective way.

Chapter 2

A Leader's Road Map

The twenty-eight-day course outlined in this book is based on a new model of leadership development and a new way of thinking about leadership itself. This model is based on the capacity of each person to create a fulfilling life by contributing his or her talents, skills, and passion to make necessary change in his or her life and in the world. This process of leadership is an unending spiral that takes everyone through the challenges and victories in our lives and moves us upward into greater understanding and service and ultimately greater leadership impact. As you put these learnings into practice in your life, you will find that they will serve you in all sorts of ways on your journey and help you stay focused on what matters most—your leadership potential.

The Leadership Model for Change has seven stages:

1. **Authentic Self.** Learning who you are is an ongoing process of self-reflection and discovery. At this stage you learn what your unique talents, skills, and passions are and how to effectively communicate them to others.

2. **Desired Change**. What is the change you wish to create in your life? This step helps you focus on your passion and what it is you wish to do *now* so that you can succinctly and clearly articulate it to others.

3. **Alignment of Purpose**. Is your life and the way you are living it supportive of who you are and what you want to do? At this point, you will reflect on *your* life and determine if you are really walking your talk.

4. **Leadership Skills.** While each person is unique, there are certain skill sets that are important for leadership. At this stage you will focus on cultivating key qualities necessary for taking your leadership into the world.

5. **Creating a Team.** No one accomplishes change by themselves. During this step you will learn how to most effectively engage others in your leadership.

6. **Real World Results**. Leadership doesn't work unless you're putting it into action to create change. This stage helps you realize when you have reached your goals and how to look toward the next step on your journey.

7. **Reflect and Refocus**. Making the Leadership Choice is not a once-in-a-lifetime decision—it is one that you make over and over again. This stage is about reflecting on where you have been and what you have learned and then making the commitment to start the journey again.

The twenty-eight-day course takes you through each of the stages focusing on creating real-world results. The final chapter of this book provides suggestions on how to use these learnings to continue your leadership journey. The lessons embodied in the twenty-eight-days are timeless and will hopefully be ones that you will return to again and again. While the details may change, you will find that the essence of who you are and your leadership skills will remain the same as you move forward in your life.

Part II

The Twenty-Eight-Day Course

Guiding Thought for the Day

Each moment within each day we are sending powerful messages to ourselves and to others through our thoughts. For each day of this course, I offer a thought for you to repeat to yourself to help anchor the day's lesson into your thought patterns. This process will help you get rid of ineffective patterns that may be keeping you from being the leader you wish to be.

Journal Exercise

The practice of writing in our own hand is becoming a lost art in our electronic age. While fully engaging in our technological era is an integral part of leadership, this course asks you to spend time each day on exercises that need to be completed by putting pen to paper. Since you will likely want to revisit these lessons often on your leadership journey, I suggest that you get a new journal, pad of paper, or book in which you will enjoy writing throughout the course (and hopefully beyond). As an additional motivator, find a pen you like and save it for these exercises only.

Leadership Skills: Taking Action

Leadership requires great strength of the mind and spirit, but even more importantly, it requires action. Each day in this course you will be asked to take some action to practice the leadership lesson being discussed. Some may continue over many days, though in almost all cases, the activities will not require inordinate amounts of time. They will, however, ask you to push your comfort zones, they may press against long-held beliefs, and they will ensure that you grow and develop your leadership in ways that will create changes in your life that you can't even begin to fathom as you embark on this journey. A leader knows he must take the next step, but he doesn't always know how the path will open once he does!

From My Experience

As you will come to understand as you take this course, everyone has a passion for service. For me, it is helping people understand their talents and skills and how to best put them out into the world. Each day, I offer insights from my more than twenty years of coaching, teaching, and speaking about these ideas with others. The theme behind each piece of wisdom is that what we share as humans is so much greater than anything that seems to separate us. The emotions you will experience during this course, and the trials and tribulations you have endured to this point in your life are shared by many. By learning how others have moved beyond their challenges, so too will you, and hopefully with much greater grace and ease.

This course is the core of my life's work. It is my sincere hope that you will find these lessons valuable in developing your leadership skills and that you will feel empowered to take your gifts confidently into the world, as your leadership is needed now more than ever.

Day 1

Living the Leadership Choice

Photo by Michael Iskowitz

Guiding Thought for the Day

By choosing to be a leader, I own my ability to change my world.

As you think about today's lesson, repeat the thought above to yourself throughout the day, knowing that the more confident you become, the more effective you will be in leading and changing your world.

Journal Exercise

Begin your journal exercise by writing the Guiding Thought for the Day at the top of your page. Next, spend at least three minutes answering the following questions in your own hand.

Why do you want to lead? What draws you to the study of leadership?

Please do not spend a lot of time thinking about your answer before beginning to write. The goal of this exercise is to understand your true thoughts and feelings without the filters so many of us have learned to use when communicating about ourselves.

Once you have completed the answer to the question above, spend at least two minutes answering this question:

Why have you not led in the way you wanted up to this point in your life?

Leadership Skills: Taking Action

"Be the change you wish to see in the world."—Gandhi

Each person has the ability, indeed the "response-ability" to change our world for the better. Despite this, so few of us actually take the initiative do it. It is far easier to sit back and blame others for not acting or to be angry about the actions of others than to truly engage ourselves in the process of change. It can be messy and challenging, and it requires us to put ourselves out there. Today's action is about testing your ability to change the way you lead—even in a small way.

As you go through your day today, look for three opportunities to respond to people differently that will change the situation. Is someone at your office upset about something? Instead of joining in the complaint session, ask the person what it would take to change things, and then suggest a concrete action for him to take. Does the barista at the local coffee shop have a bad attitude? Take a moment to compliment her on something she is doing well. Do you have a friend or family member who can't seem to get out of his own way? Suggest an action that can move him forward without indulging his inertia.

After you have engaged in each of the three opportunities to change *your* interactions in these daily life situations, reflect on the power of your ability to *lead* and change your world by simply shifting how you engage in a situation.

From My Experience

Every one of us is so much more powerful than we give ourselves credit for. When coaching clients, I find that the first step is helping them recognize their capacity to create change, even if at first it is in small ways. So much joy and excitement is unleashed when people start to see themselves as empowered.

Most institutions in our Western societies teach us that belief in ourselves is misplaced. We must have someone tell us what to do, think, or say. One essential element of effective leadership is learning to trust ourselves and the power that each of has to contribute to the betterment of our organizations, neighborhoods, communities, and lives.

Day 2

Cultivating Self-Awareness and the Journey of Self-Discovery

Photo by Kathleen Schafer

Guiding Thought for the Day

I am aware of my thoughts, and I have the power to choose them.

As you think about today's lesson, repeat the thought above to yourself or out loud throughout the day. As you become aware of your thoughts and the choices you are making with each thought you will begin to see the potential for shifting old patterns and making new leadership choices.

Journal Exercise

Begin your journal exercise by writing the Guiding Thought for the Day at the top of your page. Next, spend at least three minutes answering the following question in your own hand:

What do you believe to be true about your ability to lead?

Again, do not spend a lot of time thinking about your answer before beginning to write.

Once you have completed the answer to the question above, spend a few minutes reviewing your answer and put your responses into two columns: in the first, put the empowered thoughts you have and in the second, list those responses that identify the limitations or barriers that prevent you from leading right now. Once you have the two lists, answer the following questions:

What can you do to amplify the positive reasons for your leadership success? What shifts in your thinking do you need to make to change barriers into opportunities?

Leadership Skills: Taking Action

"He who looks outside his own heart dreams, he who looks inside his own heart, awakens."—Carl Jung

Fundamentally, each person has great strength, skills, and talents that can be brought to effect positive change in the world. Unfortunately, too many of us are taught that who we are isn't good enough, isn't right for our families or community, or will never earn us a good living. This stops many of us from connecting to our true selves because it hurts, and therefore we turn our focus outward. After all, it is much easier to blame others and outside circumstances for what isn't working in our lives.

True leadership means recognizing these patterns and changing them so that we can discover who we were born to be. This in turn allows us to unleash our power. Today's leadership action is one of self-awareness. As you interact with the various people in your life—family, friends, co-workers—look for at least three examples of where you are: denying your true desires in a situation; not bringing your talents or understanding to a situation that needs it; and feeling that you must hide parts of yourself to keep the peace.

As you become aware of not fully bringing yourself to a particular situation, ask yourself these important questions:

Can this situation be improved by your full participation? What would happen if you fully exercised your leadership?

As you did with your journal exercise, be aware of which column your responses fall into Do you see the potential for positive change as a result of becoming more authentic? Or do you feel that being yourself results in immediate disadvantages?

From My Experience

As I embarked on the leadership journey, it became clear very quickly that I needed to let go of many preconceived notions about what leadership looked like. I had learned in childhood that if I couldn't control it, it wouldn't work out that way I wanted it to ... and in too many instances with my trying to "control" it still didn't work out, because no one can control other people or situations. Continuing with that behavior wasn't leadership, as I had once thought to be true, it was a recipe for disaster.

Many people I have worked initially believed that the power to be a leader and the ability to create change was limited to others, specifically others who have achieved certain forms of external success. No one ever experiences the power of leadership until they are able to honestly look at themselves, see the beauty that is there, and believe that they are great. Believing in the real you is at the root every successful leader, and your willingness to be the leader only you can be is the way to create success.

Day 3

Who Am I?

Photo by Jason Claire

Guiding Thought for the Day

My true nature is eternal and does not change.

Repeat the thought above to yourself throughout the day as you become aware that your true nature is not defined by the roles you play (e.g., employee, spouse, parent, volunteer, etc.), but rather by the unchanging qualities you bring to these roles (e.g., loving, understanding, insightful, etc.).

Journal Exercise

Begin your journal exercise by writing the Guiding Thought for the Day at the top of your page. Next, spend at least three minutes answering the following question:

Who are you?

The goal of this exercise is to get as deep as you can about what makes you *you*.

Now spend a few minutes reviewing your answer and identify what qualities can be easily changed and what qualities will never change. Once you have the two lists, answer the following question:

How can you more effectively bring your eternal qualities to the various roles you play in life?

Leadership Skills: Taking Action

"Those who are firm, enduring, simple, and unpretentious are the nearest to virtue."—Confucius

Who am I? Never has there been such a simple question that elicits such complex feelings. For many, their initial response begins with the identification of labels and roles we have been given by others (e.g., child, student, parent, friend, coworker, boss, spouse, sibling, or volunteer). Yet these are not the things that make us who we are! What makes you who you are is the part of yourself that remains unchanged in *all* the various role you play in your life.

When we over-identify with the roles we have taken on, we cede control over our lives to external sources and move away from our true source of power. If maintaining a title, a job, or some other position becomes your definition of yourself, then keeping that position becomes paramount. Now not only has your power been lost—so too has your focus because trying to keep something that is fleeting is a frivolous pursuit. When you fully indentify with who you truly are, you build your life and your leadership on those qualities that are unchanging.

Indentifying your leadership qualities is the focus of your work during the next few days. Today you continue to reflect on your true nature—what is it that you bring to the world that no one else does? What are the enduring qualities you possess regardless of the role or situation? By becoming aware of your true source of power, you begin building your life of leadership on firm ground—ground that does not change as your life changes, but rather supports you regardless of what you build upon it.

From My Experience

When I was first asked this question, I got mad. What difference does it make who *I* am? Can't everyone see that I have worked hard and accomplished all these wonderful things that define my worth? I had finally accumulated all this stuff, all these accolades, and now you want me to consider the thought that it was all worthless? Preposterous!

Well, like so much of this leadership journey, the truth is often quite humbling. Certainly I had some great achievements and possessions that reflected success, but as with so much in life, at some point they had become meaningless because I had not acquired them for the right reasons. I believed that amassing external reflections of success made me worth something. In time I realized that anything on the outside can be taken away in a moment by unexpected circumstances or situations that have nothing to do with my actions. (We need look no further than the past few years to see examples of this everywhere in our world from natural to manmade disasters.) So if this is the case, then the source of my power must be elsewhere, because even in adversity, I still had me.

As I came to grips with the reality that external achievements and possessions can vanish in an instant, I came back to this simple question: Who am I? In taking the time to fully answer it, I discovered a source of strength I never knew I had—as a woman who is rarely accused of being a shrinking violet that is saying a great deal! For me, this question was indeed the beginning of my journey to understand where true power lies and to build a life on firm ground rather than shifting sands.

Day 4

What Are My Talents, Strengths, and Abilities?

Photo by Kathleen Schafer

Guiding Thought for the Day

I possess great talents and strengths.

Repeat the thought above to yourself throughout the day as you work to become aware of the many amazing, wonderful talents and strengths you bring to the world. An effective leader must fully own the gifts he or she has to give.

Journal Exercise

Begin your journal exercise by writing the Guiding Thought for the Day at the top of your page. Next, spend at least three minutes answering the following questions:

What are your natural talents? What do you love doing that is simply fun and easy for you to do?

Please do not spend a lot of time thinking about your answer before beginning to write. The goal of this exercise is to get past the barriers of what you think you should be to find out who you truly are.

Once you have completed the answer to the questions above, spend a few minutes reviewing your answer and circle the top three skills that you feel truly represent your best qualities.

Leadership Skills: Taking Action

"When I stand before God at the end of my life, I would hope that I would not have a single bit of talent left and could say, 'I used everything you gave me.'"—Erma Bombeck

As you begin to own your leadership talents and strengths, the challenge becomes how to identify and describe them so that others can easily understand and connect with you. To help with this process, I have identified a variety of leadership assessment tools useful in developing a specific context for understanding how your strengths relate to other people's leadership talents. This is important when you communicate with others as well as later in the course when we focus on the importance of teamwork in your leadership endeavors.

Three accessible leadership assessment tools are:

- Keirsey Type Sorter Assessment: www.keirsey.com
- Enneagram: www.enneagraminstitute.com
- StrengthsFinder: www.strengthsfinder.com

At each of these sites you will find free on-line assessments as well as fee-based options. In addition, each of these tools offers books that explain the assessment styles in great detail for those of you looking for deeper insight and understanding. Today your task is to begin to understand your leadership style by visiting at least one of these sites and completing the assessment tool of your choice. Take time to reflect on what each one says about the leader you are.

From My Experience

Often when I ask people if they have taken a leadership assessment tool like Myers-Briggs, I am met with a look of terror or a groan of displeasure as they remember being told in high school that they were destined for some dreary vocation based on the results. If only taken at face value, these tools are often mistakenly used to put people into boxes—and who wants to feel as if their options in life are limited?

I prefer Don Riso's take on these assessments. Founder of the contemporary Enneagram, Riso says, "Our goal is not to put you into a box; rather, it is to help you understand the one you are already in and help you get out of it." So many people haven't considered the idea that there is an entire spectrum of human behavior and leadership qualities that vary from person to person—indeed that there is no right or wrong way to lead. Someone who is very organized is not better than someone who prefers to keep things open-ended. What is important is to understand your tendencies and be able to identify the tendencies of others. People approach leadership, communication, and work differently. By knowing your style, you are better able to participate with a group, and by recognizing other styles, you can help others to do the same—that is leadership.

Day 5

What Am I Truly Passionate About?

Photo by Jason Claire

Guiding Thought for the Day

My passions guide me to greater fulfillment and happiness.

Repeat the thought above to yourself throughout the day as you become aware that there are certain things in life that you love to do. I am talking about the things that are effortless, where you lose track of time and experience a fulfillment and happiness that you don't experience anywhere else. These are the things to (re)discover in your life to fuel your leadership potential.

Journal Exercise

Begin your journal exercise by writing the Guiding Thought for the Day at the top of your page. Next, spend at least three minutes answering the following question.

At five years old, what did you want to be when you grew up and why?

Many people can remember wanting to be a teacher, a doctor, or even the president. These are all good answers, but I want you to go deeper. Why did you want to be a teacher? Because your mother, aunt, or favorite person was a teacher? Why was that important to you? Did you like they way she helped people feel good about themselves? Were you attracted to the orderliness of the classroom? Did you like the fun you can have with a group of children? Why did this matter to you? What is the essence of why you wanted to play that role? What was the passion that sparked your fire?

After you have answered the question and asked yourself why at least three times to get to the essence of your desire—write down what that passion is about. Once you have completed this step, ask yourself when you began to feel as if your passion wasn't good enough to pursue? Who communicated to you that what you wanted to do wouldn't earn you a good living or wasn't what a "successful" person would do with his or her life?

Leadership Skills: Taking Action

"A great leader's courage to fulfill his vision comes from passion, not position."—John Maxwell

Passion is a word we hear about in relation to leadership, but too often it is dismissed as an ephemeral characteristic having much more to do with amorous emotions. The definition of passion is "a strong and barely controllable emotion," or "an intense desire or enthusiasm for something." Both have significance for your effectiveness as a leader. Having strong (positive) emotions about your work in the world is critical for its success. Too many people have allowed themselves to be caught in jobs that they never loved or no longer love because it pays the bills, or it would be too hard to find another job, or it was what they always thought they wanted to do. If passion is not a central part of your work each day, and if you can't honestly say, "I love what I am doing," then perhaps it is time to consider another way.

When you start thinking about what else you might do, consider the second definition of passion. What is it that you have an intense desire or enthusiasm for? (In coming lessons we will focus on the change element of this question.) Today I ask you to identify what is it that makes you feel alive. What do you want to do above all other things? If you are uncertain, go back and have this conversation with your five-year-old self.

From My Experience

When I ask people during a coaching session what they wanted to be when they grew up at five years of age, they often give me a sheepish grin and then begin thinking about how they can make the answer sound impressive. After all, they have learned well that some ambitions have merit and value and others are foolish and impractical. It's interesting how society squelches the natural enthusiasm of a child and quite sad when you can identify with the kid who had someone pour a bucket of cold water on their beautiful fire.

Now is the time to begin looking at your true self and your passion not through the eyes of the socialized adult but through the eyes of the child who saw a world of possibilities. While mature sensibilities are important to living our passion and leadership in the world, if we can't find the genius of our true selves, we will never be capable of fueling our ambitions. If we keep the focus on the external reasons for our success (e.g., money, power, fame, etc.), then we have handed the reins of our future over to other people who I guarantee have very different ideas about what you can and can't achieve. By opening up to the passion you came into the world to express, you have begun to tap into a great power that no one can take away from you!

Day 6

What Makes Me Unique?

Photo by Karin Heinzl

Guiding Thought for the Day

I am unique. I have something to offer the world that no one else does.

For today's lesson, repeat the thought above to yourself as you think about how you are unique and have a powerful contribution to make in the world. Equally important is to understand that everyone has a something valuable to offer. Uniqueness is not about creating a pecking order among people—it is about honoring the amazing confluence of talents, skills, and passions that each individual possesses. Herein lies the key to your leadership—knowing what it is you bring to the world, expressing it clearly, and allowing other people who share mutual interests to support you.

Journal Exercise

Begin your journal exercise by writing the Guiding Thought for the Day at the top of your page. Next, spend at least three minutes answering the following questions in your own hand:

What makes you unique? What can you bring to the world that no one else can?

For all the times we have been told not to toot our own horns, we have forgotten how to connect to the bright spot in us that is different than anyone else's. Let me be clear that I am not asking you to come up with reasons why you are better than everyone else. I am asking you to identify the qualities in yourself that make you who you are. Nobody would argue that each person *looks* different from everyone else, so why should we feel that we can't *be* different from everyone else? And just like in our appearance, some people are similar and others are very unlike us. However, when put together, our differences and similarities compliment one another, coming together like pieces in a puzzle to make the world complete.

After you have answered the questions, review your answer and sum up your writing in a few sentences. That is, how can you communicate your uniqueness to another person in less than thirty seconds? Use your talents, skills, and passion to create a quick and easy way for you to share with others your leadership qualities.

Leadership Skills: Taking Action

"First organize the inner, then organize the outer . . . first organize the great, then organize the small . . . first organize yourself, then organize others."—Zhuge Liang

Leaders organize themselves by understanding what makes them unique. Until you identify your authentic self, it is difficult to effectively more forward to the other stages of leadership, or as Liang puts it "to organize others." While this exercise may feel frivolous and self-indulgent, it is an important part of leadership to know your unique value and learn how to remain humble in the presence of others and their equally important unique qualities.

When you own your uniqueness and are able to easily communicate it to others, you can begin living the process of leadership. You are showing your authentic self to others in a way that values your talents and strengths and that allows others the opportunity to do the same. There is no more powerful gift one can give than to acknowledge the spark of uniqueness in another. Once this is understood, leaders are able to move forward easily attracting people to their cause. For today, practice expressing your authentic self to others.

From My Experience

While you may feel uncomfortable about discussing your uniqueness at first, there is nothing more amazing to witness than a person who suddenly recognizes their special gifts. I have seen incredible and immediate transformations in people who realize that they don't need to work for years or achieve a certain position to have value; what is valuable about them is inside and has nothing to do with the role they are playing at that moment.

Imagine the power of experiencing that moment yourself. What would the world look like if you owned your unique talents and decided that nothing was going to stop you from offering it to the world? As a favorite author of mine, Marianne Williamson, says, "Our deepest fear is not that we are inadequate. Our deepest fear is that we are powerful beyond measure." We fear not what we can't do, but the prospect of actually doing what we know we can, because our lives have been built around not allowing ourselves to be and experience all we can. In this way, leadership is about being a living example of being all you can be.

Day 7

What Do I Really Want?

Photo by Kathleen Schafer

Guiding Thought for the Day

I can be and have all I desire.

As you think about today's lesson, repeat the thought above to yourself. Internalize the idea that you are limitless—all barriers to achieving your desires are easily removed by identifying what you truly want. So many people become confused when they focus only on external goals as justification for their existence and success. By clearly identifying what you want most, you fill your life with the important elements first and then the secondary expressions of happiness and impact come much more easily.

Journal Exercise

Begin your journal exercise by writing the Guiding Thought for the Day at the top of your page. Next, spend at least three minutes answering the following question:

What do you want in your life?

List everything from the new red sports car to quality relationships to the vacation of a lifetime—don't filter any of your responses, just let them come. As long as you have a new desire, write it down.

After you have finished your list, close your eyes, relax for a few moments, and connect to what you have just done. Hopefully you will experience a sense of joy for allowing yourself to express what you would like in your life. Now review the list and circle the three most important things you want. In other words, if you could only have three things on your list, what do you most want to create in your life? These will be the three things on which your leadership actions will first be focused.

Leadership Skills: Taking Action

"Nothing so conclusively proves a man's ability to lead others as what he does from day-to-day to lead himself."—Thomas J. Watson

As a follow-up to the adage that it is impossible to hit a target you don't know exists, so many people live their lives without truly understanding what it is they want. What do you want to change in the world? What do you want to experience? What kind of quality of life do you want? Everyone has desires, and yet few of us take the time to really identify where and what we want to create in our lives. Without focused desire, one of two things usually happens: either we set out on a path that doesn't lead to where we want to go, or we obtain what it is that we want but because we aren't focused on it, we don't realize when we have hit our mark.

There is an amazing power and sense of empowerment that comes when you identify what really matters to you. It provides focus, direction, and purpose to your life and your work. Defining your wants clarifies where you are going and allows you to easily communicate it to others so that they can decide to join you or not. Clarity makes life easier. By clearly identifying your wants, you have provided the foundation for establishing goals, achieving tangible results, making life successful and a lot more fun! Today's exercise is to become clear about the three changes you want to start working on—now.

From My Experience

Knowing what we want in life is harder than most people think. I have a friend who once likened the experience to ordering dinner at a restaurant. When presented with a list of options, most of us are able to make a selection and allow the request to be met. Few people change their minds after they place their order because they have made the best selection based on the options given them. Life, however, doesn't work that way. There is no prescribed menu for you—it is up to you to create your list, and it requires even more focus to remain confident in your order until it arrives.

How many times have you wanted something, then hit a roadblock and decided to go a different direction? How often have you been dissuaded from pursuing your dreams because someone told you it could never happen? When were those moments that you knew you wanted to pursue something but didn't because the path was unclear?

The first step in achieving anything, particularly as a leader, is to believe that you can be it, have it, and do it. The second is to make the commitment to pursue what matters to you regardless of what the outside world tells you is and isn't possible. And finally, as you hold on to your vision, you build energy around it by allowing others to come to you with their support. Easy or hard—it is all a matter of perspective.

Day 8

Understanding the Contribution I Want to Make

Photo by Karin Heinzl

Guiding Thought for the Day

Contributing my talents and skills to supporting others fulfills my life's purpose.

As you think about today's lesson, repeat the thought above to yourself and focus on the idea that fulfillment comes from enriching the lives of others. What is it that you can contribute to the world? Yesterday you identified what you want in life; today focus on what change you wish to make in the world.

Journal Exercise

Begin your journal exercise by writing the Guiding Thought for the Day at the top of your page. Next, spend at least three minutes answering the following question:

If you could change one thing in the world, what would it be?

I know it is difficult to think about what you would change, so to make this work, and I encourage you to challenge yourself with this question. Another way to think about it is to ask yourself, *If I could wave a magic wand and change something in the world, what would it be?* Write down everything that comes to you.

After you have finished writing, review your answer to find the key theme. Look beyond your answer to identify what it is that *you* want to change that will ultimately contribute to achieving your goal? What is it that *you* can contribute that no one else can?

Leadership Skills: Taking Action

"Change is hard because people overestimate the value of what they have—and underestimate the value of what they may gain by giving that up."—James Belasco and Ralph Stayer

What do you want to change in the world? That question usually conjures up a host of answers about sweeping reforms in the world and ideas that generally have to do with global change. It is wonderful that so many people see the need for improvements throughout the world, although the challenge of identifying with this level of change is that it leaves the responsibility for creating the change to someone else. Clearly one person living an ordinary life can't possibly have impact on global warming, world peace, or the United States' tax structure. This is exactly the train of thought that keeps people from taking action—and it is what distinguishes leaders from others. It is the leader who looks for a way to start creating change *now*.

Leaders learn to take their passion for change and break it down into actionable pieces that they pursue right away. The steps they take are rooted in their talents and skills, fueled by their passion, and put on track with the change they want to create. This leads to a trajectory that will inevitably have a profound impact on the world. True, it may not change the world overnight, and we must realize that no one and nothing ever has. While some change feels like it occurred instantaneously, the reality is that all change takes time—from the genesis of the idea, to the first steps, to the determination that finally leads to the tipping point of mass momentum, and *finally* change. Study any leader who championed a change in the world and you will find someone who spent years working toward that change, even if to you it looked as if it were natural and effortless. Your change will feel like that at some point—that is if you take the time to put it into motion today.

From My Experience

I can't tell you how many clients have looked at me like I'm crazy when I suggest that they have the ability to change the world. As one who is forever quoting Margaret Mead and her priceless insight, "Never doubt that a small group of people can change the world; indeed, it is the only thing that ever does," I am a firm believer in the power of a leader who is aligned with his or her values to truly make a profound impact on our world.

Unfortunately, so many of us get caught in common traps. For some, it is the false belief that change only happens when a person is in a position of power. The fact is, most leaders who have created real change did so when they were *not* in a formal position but purely as a result of their leadership skills. For others, it is feeling that if something can't be accomplished overnight, it won't work or it isn't worth doing. In Malcolm Gladwell's *The Outliers*, he documents how true masters become so only after ten thousand hours of practicing their craft. What he's saying is that true change is not for the faint of heart but rather for those with the perseverance to create the change in themselves as they create it for others.

Whatever is keeping you from moving forward toward your change goals and putting the best of yourself into the world is likely an excuse. Remember that what you fear is not failure; rather, it is the lack of belief in the bounty of what it is you can accomplish by putting your vision of change to work in the world today.

Day 9

Giving My Best to Family and Friends

Photo by Kathleen Schafer

Guiding Thought for the Day

Giving my best to those with whom I am the closest is the foundation of my leadership.

Repeat the thought above to yourself throughout the day as you focus on how you conduct yourself with those who mean the most to you. Too often we reserve our best behavior for those outside our inner circle—this only reinforces the notion that we should build an external façade instead of cultivating an authentic life where our inner and outer expressions are the same. Today, focus on giving your best to those you love and expanding your influence from there.

Journal Exercise

Begin your journal exercise by writing the Guiding Thought for the Day at the top of your page. Next, spend at least three minutes answering the following question:

How can you shift your interactions with your family and friends to be a more authentic reflection of who you are?

The greatest contribution you have to give the world is you. And if you can't be who you are with *all* the people you love and are closest to you, it is impossible for you to fully be yourself with everyone else. What parts of yourself have you been hiding? What is it about you that you don't share with others? Why? How can you lovingly express yourself without being attached to how others respond to you?

After you have finished writing what you can do different to fully express yourself within your circle of family and friends, write the answer to these questions: *What has stopped you from authentically expressing yourself? What can be gained by changing your interactions with this group? What changes will you bring to their lives as a result of fully expressing yourself as the leader you are?*

Leadership Skills: Taking Action

"Leadership is not so much about technique and methods as it is about opening the heart. Leadership is about inspiration—of oneself and of others. Great leadership is about human experiences, not processes. Leadership is not a formula or a program, it is a human activity that comes from the heart and considers the hearts of others. It is an attitude, not a routine."—Lance Secretan

For so many people aspiring to great leadership in the world, the thought of change often pertains to the vast world stage. As I have discussed, though it can be a daunting prospect to begin such an endeavor, it can be equally terrifying to think about changing and truly revealing ourselves to those with whom we are closest. Yet if you are to begin walking the path of leadership, it starts at home and with your conduct around those with whom you share your life. This is the foundation of you and your leadership, so how you interact with loved ones is the soil that nourishes all else you will plant in your life.

What is it that you have to give to this vitally important group of people? How can you begin to enjoy your talents and strengths by sharing them with those you love the most? What is it in your interactions with family and friends that have contributed to the person you have become? What is it time to let go of? And what needs to be celebrated?

For whatever reason, your family and close friends are a part of your life to help you become the leader you can be. With some, it was their love and support that have helped you, for others it may have been their irritating qualities that have led you to see and express valuable parts of yourself. Regardless, the time has come for you to consciously be your authentic self with this group, to express yourself honestly and contribute positively to the group dynamics. Not everyone will respond in kind, and that's okay—the only person you have control over is you. And as you lead and create change within yourself, your leadership journey will begin where it must—at home.

Today, start putting your leadership to work in the world by shifting your contribution to those with whom you are closest . . . and begin to see things change.

From My Experience

No matter how varied or different our familial experiences have been, every one of us is impacted each day by our history with this important group of people. Whether they were fully present in your life, not present enough, not present at all, or not there in the way you may have wanted—your experiences with close family and friends have shaped your understanding of yourself. As each of us steps onto the leadership path, it is important to take note of our abilities as individuals to own the narrative of our lives and be authors of our stories.

The first step on the path of authenticity is to take ownership of your true self and no longer allow others to define you. You have something to contribute to your family and the world, and the first place for you to revel in who you are is with your family. From there you learn the lessons you need to take into the world. Some will support you, some may mock you, others will remain silent and aloof. All of this is okay, as each person has the right to his or her feelings and you don't need to buy into everything someone else thinks. The key lesson to be learned and practiced with your family first is that leadership is not about getting everyone to like you and/or to do what you want. Leadership is about being your best self, offering your talents to others, and going where you are invited to share your gifts.

There is no better practice ground than your home turf, and if you can live it with your family and friends, you can live your leadership anywhere in the world!

Day 10

What Can I Bring to the Organizations in Which I Volunteer and Work?

Photo by Karin Heinzl

Guiding Thought for the Day

I create change each day that I am aware of my power to change myself.

The only place you can truly create change is within you. You cannot change anyone else. Therefore, the power to create change rests solely within you and your capacity to shift your conduct, which then will create a different response in those around you. That is the essence of leadership. It is not in the telling of others what to do, but rather it is in being your best self and inspiring those around you to do the same.

Journal Exercise

Begin your journal exercise by writing the Guiding Thought for the Day at the top of your page. Next, spend at least three minutes answering the following question:

What change do you want to create in the organizations in which you volunteer and work?

For today's exercise, it may be helpful to list the organizations in which you are actively involved. It can be your workplace, place of worship, volunteer or school organizations. Any group with which you are involved already has one of your most precious resources—your time and attention—and therefore deserves your focus on what you have to contribute as a result of your participation.

After you have finished with your organization list and the desired changes, select the one organization you want to focus on right away. Now make a list of short-term change goals that you can accomplish *within the next three months*. For each of those goals, identify objectives that can be accomplished *within the next three weeks*. Lastly, for each of those objectives, identify a step that can be taken *today and for the next three days* that will put you on the path to achieving your goals.

Leadership Skills: Taking Action

"All is connected . . . no one thing can change by itself."—Paul Hawken

Creating change in your organizations doesn't have to be about radical shifts and interventions. The change you are seeking may be to create greater civility and respect for one another, which is a terrific goal for those who are seeking world peace, because it is difficult to achieve peace in the world if you are participating in an acrimonious work environment. In fact, it is those small initial shifts that gradually open the door to greater and greater levels of positive change. Because we are all connected, the awareness you bring to being fully present in your leadership allows others to feel permission to do the same.

As you begin the process of creating change in your work environment, be prepared to articulate to others the values you are bringing to this process. Following the above example, you may say during a heated staff meeting, "I realize the importance of respecting a variety of opinions on how to create the best product, and *I* am going to do a better job listening to varying points of view." It may seem like a small step, yet by simply stating how you are committed to conducting yourself, you are offering others a choice to do the same. Today, look for opportunities to make these small changes in your organization.

From My Experience

If you want to make someone uncomfortable, ask him or her to clearly express himself or herself in front of coworkers. While our families provide ample opportunity to learn to navigate the internal roadblocks we have created for ourselves, authentically dealing with coworkers puts the "public persona" we have so carefully crafted to the test. What is it about yourself that you don't want to show other people? Do you fear that you won't "know it all"? Are you worried someone will discover that there are some things you are not as proficient in or enjoy?

The beauty of learning to articulate your talents and strengths and share them with others in the process of change is that you are free to be yourself. As a human, you naturally *can't* be good at everything. For instance, the detail-oriented person loves minutiae and is good at keeping it organized. It makes sense that he or she wouldn't be the person with the big-picture ideas. When you begin seeking change and improvement, what naturally occurs is the need to have people with a variety of talents involved, which is the first step toward accepting a variety of skills and developing an understanding about how to put them to the best use to achieve the group's goal.

Day 11

What Change Do I Wish to See in My Community?

Photo by Jason Claire

Guiding Thought for the Day

My community is a reflection of me; as I bring my best to the community, my community becomes better.

Your ability to create change can have an immediate impact on your community. Each one of us has great potential to make things better, even by doing small things differently. It is difficult when we focus on the negative and allow ourselves to feel unempowered. Today, focus on what you want to happen and do something to move in that direction—and then pay attention to the feeling it creates in you.

Journal Exercise

Begin your journal exercise by writing the Guiding Thought for the Day at the top of your page. Next, spend at least three minutes answering the following questions:

What change do you want to create in your community? What would feel good to see improved?

Thinking about community change can make our thoughts a bit fuzzy, and often our intention wanes because, after all, what effect can one person really have? Yet our communities are the context in which we live our lives, and if we're not conscious of the world in which we live, we close ourselves off to so many wonderful possibilities to put our leadership into practice. In today's exercise, identify *no more than three* things you want to shift in your community. Then, beside each item, write *at least three* actions you can take to bring it into reality.

Levels of Community

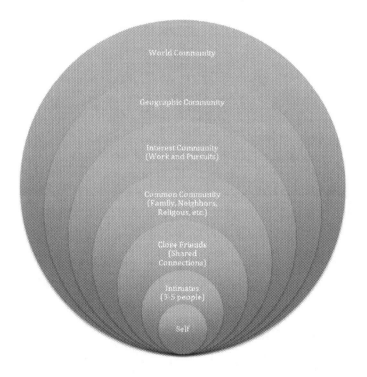

Leadership Skills: Taking Action

"Once there is seeing, there must be acting. Otherwise, what is the use of seeing?"—Thich Nhat Hanh

Community change brings another layer of complexity to your leadership and walking it in the world, because now you must come into contact with people with whom you don't know. Now you must truly begin to engage the skills of revealing your authentic self to others, which can be challenging when they are strangers. Yet with how many "strangers" do you interact each day? Begin with your morning and think through your day, from the barista at the coffee shop or your children's bus driver to the grocery store clerk, your doctor, or your letter carrier. Each one of these people comprises a piece of your community, and yet so many of us are oblivious to the impact we can have on them and the impact they have on us. What is the quality of that connection? What is the quality of community?

In the *Seven Circles of Community* (see chart), the circles important for today's lesson are the Interest Communities in which we live, work, and follow our pursuits (e.g., neighborhoods, religious groups, and schools), and the Geographic Communities, which are the larger communities around us (e.g., towns, counties, and states). These two layers of community have direct impact on our quality of life and are a direct reflection of our values and the values of those around us. By focusing your intention to be conscious of how you are leading in these spheres, you can begin to shape to the outcome of the policies, norms, and practices of those with whom you most closely share your world. Again, once you see something, you have the power to change it, and leadership is how you do it.

From My Experience

Interestingly, many people view community as the most difficult area to change, but it is actually the easiest. People either get caught up in their closest and most intimate relationships with family and friends or they focus their attention on larger world issues, such as climate change, poverty, and equality. While these are all excellent areas to improve (and the focus of tomorrow's lesson), these broad issues can be addressed only by seeing and changing what is right in front of you. If you are concerned with global poverty issues, what are you doing to address the needs of the poor in your community?

This level of change brings us face to face with the reality of leadership. Using your leadership skills in your local community means you are putting your notions about yourself, your leadership, and your capabilities to the test. As with so many things in life, there will be times to step forward and times when you will assume smaller roles. The goal of today's activity is to get you focused on the importance of community in your life and your ability to lead right where you are.

Day **12**

What Can I Do to Improve the World?

Photo by Jason Claire

Guiding Thought for the Day

My conscious commitment to leading every day allows me to change the world step by step.

Repeat the thought above to yourself throughout the day as you honor the power of your ability to change the world. Each one of us dreams of having a global impact, of sharing the best of ourselves on a world stage. This is true in part because the lure of celebrity is great, but at a deeper level it is because at our core we wish to make the world a better place. If you are like most, you have been taught that the power to change the world comes at the end of a life of external accomplishment. Today honor the power you already have just by being the leader you already are.

Journal Exercise

Begin your journal exercise by writing the Guiding Thought for the Day at the top of your page. Next, spend at least three minutes answering the following questions:

What can you shift in yourself that will create the change you wish to see in the world? How can you be the change you wish to see in the world?

Change doesn't take place "out there." It takes place internally. What is it in you that needs to shift in order to create a ripple effect? Just as the butterfly effect, which is at the root of the chaos theory, reveals how one flap of a butterfly's wing can change the weather around the world, what is the one shift that you can make that will send its powerful effects throughout our planet?

Leadership Skills: Taking Action

"There can be no happiness if the things we believe in are different than the things we do."—Albert Camus

When we look at the world, it's easy to see all the problems, challenges, and issues that must be addressed. However, looking at the world and seeing what you can do to change things is an entirely different story. It is much easier to affirm our powerlessness than to take responsibility for our role in the world. You may not be a world leader, a captain of business, or a sports hero, but you have the same ability to change a person's life as those people do. You just need to make the decision to act.

Actions of leadership are not just grand gestures imparted by those in positions of authority—in fact, these actions rarely create *real* change. Rather, leadership that changes the world consists of conscious acts made each day by individuals who see the interconnectedness of the world and know that change occurs one step at a time. Hasn't a child raised thousands of dollars to build water wells in Africa? Haven't doctors provided care to communities in natural disasters? Haven't congregations acted to support people in the developing world? Each one of these actions, taken locally, had a global impact, and for some of these people, it has become a life-changing endeavor that has created new opportunities for their leadership and quality of life. That is why living the leadership choice works—because as you offer the best you have to creating positive change and surrendering to where the path may lead, you are assured it will be in a positive direction.

From My Experience

Throughout my twenty-year career teaching leadership, the idea that each one of us can change the world has been one of the most exciting for me. When I tell this to an audience though, the general reaction is predictably pessimistic. However, with a little encouragement and discussion, most people grasp the power they have to change the world by simply focusing on what they can do each day in their lives. Some of our greatest leaders, like George Washington, Gandhi, Susan B. Anthony, and Martin Luther King, have changed the world forever simply by knowing themselves and being willing to live their beliefs in their immediate world. None of them ever could have imagined the impact their leadership would ultimately have, and it didn't matter to them. They were simply putting their passion into action.

You can do the same thing and not everyone is destined to be that type of leader. In fact, after working with thousands of people, I have met very few who actually want to live the life required of today's public leaders. People want balance in their lives, to enjoy themselves and their families, *and* they want to have an impact. The good news is that you can do it—just let go of the bigger picture and take action today!

Day **13**

Developing All Areas of My Life to Support My Leadership

Photo by Karin Heinzl

Guiding Thought for the Day

By aligning my life with my leadership intentions, I create a base of happiness and success in all my endeavors.

As you think about today's lesson, repeat the thought above to yourself or aloud throughout the day, as you connect with your power to create happiness and success in your life now. If you are focusing too much on your leadership and the impact you are having on the world, your quality of life may be suffering. The knowledge that you cannot give anything to another that you do not fully give to yourself is key to your peace and freedom, and it is essential to successfully engaging everyone with whom you come into contact.

Journal Exercise

Begin your journal exercise by writing the Guiding Thought for the Day at the top of your page. Next, spend at least three minutes answering the following questions:

How well do you take care of yourself? Are you doing the best you can do? If not, what keeps you from treating yourself in the best possible way?

Change doesn't take place "out there." It takes place internally. Why is it that those of us who spend our lives helping others often don't take time to care for ourselves? The first step in living a fully aligned life is to become conscious of our actions toward ourselves and understand what attitudes and beliefs have kept us from fully care for ourselves to this point in our lives.

Leadership Skills: Taking Action

"We don't see things as they are; we see things as we are."—Anais Nin

Today's leadership action is simply to observe yourself. You are halfway through this experience now, and you have spent a great deal of time diving into parts of yourself that may never have been fully explored, such as your talents, your passion, and the desires you have to create change in the world. All these are worthy topics and deserve the attention we have given them. Today it's time to take a breath and observe how you take care of the magnificent being you are uncovering. Just as Michelangelo had to take time to observe the marble before he carved away everything that wasn't David, the gift you can give the world today is to look at yourself and the investment you make daily in your own care.

What keeps you from loving and caring for yourself in the way that you love and care for others? What beliefs have you carried with you about your worth and happiness that you have taken on from others? And why is everyone else worthy of your wonderful attention and support but not you? These are tough but necessary questions to answer, for at the center of your response is the kernel of misperception you have internalized that have you believing that somehow you aren't good enough, smart enough, or worthy enough to have what you want for others. Until you learn to take care of yourself, you will never be capable of bringing your full power into the world. Today is the turning point. You now know the amazing qualities you have to bring into the world, and today is the day you give yourself permission to move forward with the full support of the most important person in the world—you.

From My Experience

Of all the leadership lessons I have coached, taught, lectured, and discussed during the past two decades, this lesson was the hardest for me to learn, and indeed, it is one that I return to regularly. My overwhelming desire to fix the world propelled me for many years until I hit a wall that told me I couldn't fix others, and the only one I could fix was me. Understanding why I pushed myself beyond my limits for others yet was unwilling to do the same for myself has been the greatest leadership lesson I have learned.

Once I made my care, my happiness, and my satisfaction the foundation of my world, I was finally genuinely and sincerely able to offer it to others. Each day is still a journey for me, and there are times when I stray from the path of self-care. I now know that if anything in my life has stalled, it is because I have failed to care for some part of myself—which means the only way forward is by doing what's best for me so that I can do my best for others.

Day 14

Establishing a Strong Physical Self

Photo by Kathleen Schafer

Guiding Thought for the Day

My physical body is the visual expression of me to the world.

Repeat the thought above to yourself as you focus on each decision you make in presenting yourself to the world. While we are born with a certain set of physical characteristics, we make many choices that influence how we present ourselves to the world. The more ownership you take over your physical appearance and health, the stronger presence you carry, which allows you to more effectively put your leadership into the world.

Journal Exercise

Begin your journal exercise by writing the Guiding Thought for the Day at the top of your page. Next, spend at least three minutes answering the following questions:

What is your current physical state? Is your body healthy? Are you eating well? Are you exercising? Is your presentation (e.g., grooming, clothes, mannerisms) an accurate reflection of the person you are?

On a deep level, we all understand the powerful connection between physical appearance and the qualities within a person. Try as we might, they cannot be separated. If you feel like people don't always see the value you bring, start by examining the image you are showing them.

After you have answered the questions above, write the answer to this question down:

What are three actions you can take today, to improve your physical health and visual message to the world?

Leadership Skills: Taking Action

"You must manage yourself before you can lead someone else."—Zig Ziglar

Today's leadership action focuses on recommitting to your physical vibrancy. Just as Zig Ziglar's quote expresses, it is difficult to inspire others or expect the best from them if you are not presenting it yourself. As a leader, you must exemplify the best of your physical, emotional, mental, and spiritual qualities for yourself first and for others second.

How many times have people been sidelined or given a wake-up call by a physical challenge? How often have you noticed someone's appearance and come to several conclusions about him or her in a matter of seconds? (Most studies say it takes less than five seconds for someone to form serious opinions about another.) No one can ignore his or her body and hope to be successful. Today's lesson asks you to shift your thinking about your physical well-being. Maintaining a healthy and fit body is not something you do only when you have time; it is an essential component of your overall health as well as your leadership efficacy. Following are three key areas to focus on starting today:

1. Physical Exercise:
   - Cardio—you should do some sort of aerobic exercise at least three times per week for twenty to thirty minutes.
   - Strength training—regularly use weight-bearing activities to keep your muscles toned
   - Flexibility—stretching is essential, as not being able to freely move your body is an indication of not being malleable in life. Remember, it is tree that can bend with the wind that remains standing after the storm . . . .

2. Healthy Diet
   - Eat three meals a day—skipping meals creates all kinds of challenges.
   - Eat a variety of foods—eating the same thing all the time doesn't build a strong body.
   - Discover what's best for you—investigate systems that allow you eat the foods that are best for your body type (my personal favorite is Ayurveda).

3. Pleasant Presence (you should feel good about yourself when you look in the mirror)
   - Keep up with your personal grooming, including your hairstyle (both men and women!).
   - Continuously refresh your wardrobe; adding current pieces to old favorites keeps you feeling good and your look stylish.
   - Makes sure you look put-together. We all have "pajama days" from time to time, and those moods are reflected in our appearance. To be effective, take time to look good no matter what the circumstance.

As with any change you are making in your life, if you are uncertain about the impact a particular activity may have on you, your body, or your health, be sure to talk with a professional before you begin a rigorous new regeime.

From My Experience

The topic of physical health and appearance is one of my favorites, not just because of its importance, but because of all the aspects of leadership and aligning with your purpose, it is the one in which we can actually *see* the results. At various phases and stages of your life, your physical health and appearance takes on different meanings. When we are young, our vitality seems like it will last forever. When we are in search of something, like a job or a mate, we tend to focus on how we look, and for these pursuits physical balance is driven by external circumstances. As you make the Leadership Choice in your life, your physical appearance and well-being shift from being something driven by your outer world and become much more relevant to your inner peace and power. I have always loved the spa, and for years it was an indulgence and the one place where I would allow another to care for me. As my appreciation for my physical well-being has increased, I realize that taking care of my physical health and appearance is a part of the whole person I am and the message I choose to send to the world. By looking good, I feel good, and when I feel good, the energy I communicate has a greater impact.

As you move through today's lesson, look for those things in your life that have felt like physical indulgences and see if they just may be the very things that help you on your way to a better physical quality of life.

15

Developing Effective Mental Habits

Photo by Jason Claire

Guiding Thought for the Day

My mind processes my experiences in the world; it is not the creator of my experiences.

Repeat the thought above to yourself as you focus on the difference between your thoughts and your reality. We have the power to choose our thoughts about every experience in our life (hence the Guiding Thought for the Day). As you become aware of the distinction between your thoughts and yourself, you will begin to master a power that is truly the engine of change and the foundation of every leadership success the world has witnessed.

Journal Exercise

Begin your journal exercise by writing the Guiding Thought for the Day at the top of your page. Next, spend at least three minutes answering the following question:

Are you able to witness the distinction between your thoughts and your reality? Describe the difference between the two as you experience them.

The power to change is at the core of leadership, and you cannot change without knowing there is a choice. In order to identify options, you have to identify the thoughts and not simply react to them. As you practice the identification of your thoughts, two very powerful things begin to happen. One is you will see options you never knew existed, and the other is you will become more and more connected to the you that is unending and unchangeable; that is, the true source of your leadership power and potential.

Leadership Skills: Taking Action

"He who cannot change the very fabric of his thought will never be able to change reality, and will never, therefore, make any progress."—Anwar el-Sadat

The phrase "being conscious" has become synonymous with those who posses an energy and willingness to live life differently; in many respects, it means living the life of a leader. The definition of consciousness is being aware of and responding to one's surroundings. When a leader is fully conscious, he is not just alert to what is going on around him. He knows that he has a *choice* in how he experiences what is going on *and* in how he will respond to it.

As humans have evolved, we moved from the flight-or-fight response to the reactive response as we learned to respond to various stimuli based on another's actions (e.g., if you hit me, I will hit you back). The next leap in our development is witnessing awareness. Ron Heifitz, a well-regarded leadership expert, calls this leadership characteristic "being on the balcony." In other words, people who want to change their surroundings take a moment before responding to *choose* how they will act in the next moment.

As you focus on the power of your mind and its thoughts, you will begin to recognize this vast resource that has been largely ignored. Though we are socialized from an early age to fill our brains with information, how many of us have learned that the power to choose our thoughts is truly our greatest asset? If we are able to choose how we experience something, than does it not follow that we become the master of our world as we chose the experiences that come to us?

Today's leadership activity is to become very aware of that space between stimuli and response and observe the choices *you* are making in your life. By cultivating this leadership practice every day, you will change your world because you will be making change in the most powerful place in the world—your mind.

From My Experience

As a lifelong student of human behavior, I had read about the power of the mind long ago. While the idea that my thoughts were of my own choosing made sense, I never truly grasped their power to change my experience until I spent time studying the concept and practicing it every day. After months and months of wrestling with these ideas, I came up with a simple trajectory of the mind:

- Your mind is the filter through which you make sense of the world.
- You, and all the amazing qualities that make you who you are, is *not* your mind.
- Too many of us believe our brains, minds, and thoughts are who we really are.
- If you let your mind control your thoughts, it is similar to letting your car drive you.
- *You* are the driver of your experience; take back the wheel and choose where you want to go.

Your mind is a glorious and wonderful computer that can process and create all sorts of miraculous things, but it still needs you to put in the creativity, inspiration, talent, skills, and love. By committing to being aware of what you are putting in, it will improve the quality of what is coming out. And if in every moment you choose not to allow external factors to impact the quality of your thinking, you have made a giant leap forward.

After all, just because it is raining doesn't mean there is something wrong with the car, that it will rain forever, or you are headed for an accident. Most drivers choose to believe the car will get them safely, dry, and happily to their destination. And by choosing those thoughts, it does . . . .

Day *16*

Cultivating a Healthy Emotional Core

Photo by Michael Iskowitz

Guiding Thought for the Day

My emotions are a sensor; as I tune in to my feelings, I create better feeling experiences.

Repeat this thought to yourself throughout the day as you focus on what your emotions are saying to you in each moment. So many of us have learned to deny what we are feeling and push through it because that's what we think is expected of us. To cultivate your leadership skills, you must no longer deny your feelings. True leadership comes from honoring the power of your feelings and trusting them to guide you along your path.

Journal Exercise

Begin your journal exercise by writing the Guiding Thought for the Day at the top of your page. Next, spend at least three minutes answering the following questions:

What do you do in your life currently that feels good to you? What are you doing that doesn't feel good? How often do you deny what you are feeling in order to do what you must do?

For this exercise I suggest putting your answers in three columns. For many people, the second and third columns will, unfortunately, be the longest. It is amazing how often we deny our true feelings in order to march to someone else's drum beat. Leadership excellence can never come from a person or activities that are devoid of passion and happiness. The final step in today's exercise is to answer this question:

What needs to change so that at least 95 percent of what you do in your life feels good to you?

Leadership Skills: Taking Action

"Whatever we plant in our subconscious mind and nourish with repetition and emotion will one day become a reality."—Earl Nightingale

Feeling good about our lives and ourselves has become detached from the way in which many people define success. Success is often viewed as a good job, big house, lots of toys, and all the accoutrements of what is supposed to make us happy—and yet the price of these choices is often a life and work habits that suck the joy out of our existence. Deadlines, calls, e-mails—there is always something else we should be doing, so we feel pressure and stress instead of lightness and ease.

Over time we become trained to ignore what we really want in life as that runaway car constantly tells us to keep moving, keep acquiring, and keep driving for success. At some point you have to ask why you are doing all this if you aren't enjoying yourself. If you are not happy, is anything else worth it?

People don't consciously choose to be unhappy and miserable. Most have internalized beliefs instilled in them by others that tell them they can't be happy if they don't earn a good living, have a good job, and so on. Or they have come to believe that who they are and what they love to do isn't good enough or worthy enough to pursue. So many people make choices that gradually lead them away from their passions and thus their power and capacity to be fully happy and satisfied.

One of the greatest tools for moving beyond limiting emotions is the Emotional Release Technique. As you progress through this twenty-eight-day course, a number of difficult emotions will arise as a result of your insights about who you are and why you had learned to deny your gifts. Letting go of these negative emotions will help you clear the path for greater and faster movement toward your goals.

- *Step One: Identify the Emotion.* Is it sadness? Anger? Fear? Identify it as clearly and as elaborately as you can.
- *Step Two: Observe Where You Hold This Feeling in Your Body.* Do you feel a constriction in your chest? Is your stomach upset? Fully connect to the bodily sensation and the root emotion that is causing it. Imagine yourself releasing both.
- *Step Three: Take Responsibility for Your Feelings.* You are the driver, so you have the power of choice. It is time to choose to feel better.
- *Step Four: Express Your Experience.* Take a pad of paper and begin to write down *everything* you are feeling—no editing. Write, write, and write until you feel as if you have absolutely nothing left to say on this subject.
- *Step Five: Release the Experience.* This part has two phases. First, release the physical experience by running, walking, getting a massage, or doing something that releases it from your body. Second, release the emotions by disposing of your writing, by burning it, burying it, or throwing it in a river. Just release it from your life.
- *Step Six: Share the Experience.* Find someone you trust with whom you can share what you have been through. The goal is for that person to only listen as you share your feelings—no commentary other than support.

- *Step Seven: Celebrate!* You have had the courage to release a negative pattern from your life and open up to greater joy . . . do something special for yourself. Ask yourself what would feel good, and I can assure you the first thing that comes to your mind will surprise you!

From My Experience

It is exciting for me to share the concepts of pursuing happiness in your life and the Emotional Release Technique because in my coaching work, this is where I observe the greatest shift in people. I've seen clients burst into shocked tears when I asked them what makes them happy because it had been ages since they had thought about happiness, let alone had someone ask what would feel good to them. Others have sheepishly revealed how they set aside their passions in order to fulfill someone else's notion of who they should be, only to discover anger and resentment lurking beneath the surface. And too often I have seen the despair of individuals who internalized the belief that they weren't good enough and never pursued their dreams.

The good news is that once a pattern is recognized, you have the choice to change it. While some are initially skeptical, everyone I have seen do this with sincere intention has made remarkable shifts in their lives. As you align with your purpose, you recognize the synergistic strength that comes from cultivating physical, mental, emotional, and spiritual balance. This is one of those exercises that will benefit you across the board.

Day *17*

Integrating Spiritual Practices

Photo by Karin Heinzl

Guiding Thought for the Day

That which is eternal is the true source of my power.

Repeat the thought above to yourself throughout the day as you focus on the non-physical part of yourself. As you shift your attention to the true source of power, that which is eternal, the hold the physical world has on you recedes. Money comes and goes, status, position, prestige all the old precursors to leadership have little sway over the person who is connected to his or her true source of power.

Journal Exercise

Begin your journal exercise by writing the Guiding Thought for the Day at the top of your page. Next, spend at least three minutes answering the following question:

What qualities do you possess that no one can ever take away from you?

Please do not spend a lot of time thinking about your answer before beginning to write. Simple eloquence is what is called for now. Take time to reflect on your essential and true nature—and then take another moment to marvel at its beauty.

Leadership Skills: Taking Action

"Only he who can see the invisible can do the impossible."—Frank Gaines

Today's topic is spirit, and entering into that realm often makes people uncomfortable as feelings, beliefs, and religions have provided a myriad of filters through which most people view their spiritual lives. Today I am asking that you suspend all thought and simply focus on being. You are going to take a needed break from the mind, the emotions, and your normal approach to life today to travel inward.

Regardless of one's religious beliefs, the idea of quiet reflection, contemplation, prayer, or meditation is a part of every known spiritual practice. If we are to touch on the power of the eternal, we must take the time to reach out to it. We must cultivate our ability to connect to that which does not change in us, and a quiet space is the best way to experience that presence and power. The goal of effective leadership is to carry that sense of knowing and eternal power with you in everything you do.

For some this will seem like a welcome break from the world; for others the idea of quiet reflection will feel like torture. Whatever your initial reactions, I assure you that you will be surprised by what comes out of this exercise:

- Find a quiet place where you will not be interrupted.
- Commit to doing the exercise for at least five minutes.

- Sit in a comfortable way.
- Close your eyes.
- Every time a thought comes to your mind, observe it and let it go.
- At the end of five minutes, write down what you experienced.

If you choose to take on this practice each day, you will discover the source of your power, happiness, and the most effective way to live your leadership in the world.

From My Experience

As someone who spent years priding myself on my ability to get an enormous amount of stuff accomplished in a day, the idea that sitting quietly would help me seemed ludicrous. Sure, when I had chest pains in my twenties, yoga was helpful, a nightly prayer for loved ones always seemed a good thing to do, and a moment of reflection before a speech calmed my nerves. Yet it was not until I truly yearned for my life to be everything I knew it could be that I made spiritual practice a priority.

What I have learned from my practice is that is doesn't matter how it is done or where you do it. On some days I can sit in meditation for an hour, on other days it may mean a cup of coffee watching the sunrise, and on some occasions I am called to a place of worship to connect with my higher self. In all of these experiences I have found that this is not an ending point of leadership—it is the beginning.

Tapping into wisdom will bring you a calmness and peacefulness that will ensure you can move through any storm with grace. Knowing that there is more than meets the eye helps you see past the immediate. Owning the unique talents you bring to the world gives you the courage to pursue them. Feeling a sense of peace helps you to know that everything will be all right regardless of what is happening around you in the moment. For me, these are the qualities of a true leader.

Day 18

Effective Communication and Others' Needs

Photo by Jason Claire

Guiding Thought for the Day

As I clearly communicate with others, I connect with and inspire them to do the same.

Repeat this thought above to yourself throughout the day as you focus on the importance of clearly expressing yourself to others. Remember, clear communication requires that you understand yourself and fully express it to others and that you empathize with your audience to deliver your message in a way they can hear it.

Journal Exercise

Begin your journal exercise by writing the Guiding Thought for the Day at the top of your page. Next, spend at least three minutes answering the following questions:

How effectively do you communicate with others? Are you able to communicate your authentic self in all situations? Why or why not?

As this process pivots from an internal exploration of your leadership qualities to the external path of living your leadership in the world, quality communication is the first step. Leadership cannot take place without a connection between two or more people, and it is impossible to connect with another without effective communication. Allow yourself to honestly critique your communication talents in the various circumstances in your life (e.g., one-on-one, groups, large audiences, strangers, friends, loved ones, etc.) and see where your natural inclinations lie and where you may need to take time to be more mindful of your communication style.

Leadership Skills: Taking Action

"The art of communication is the language of leadership."—James Humes

An unknown person is credited with saying, "The basic building block of good communication is the understanding that every person is unique and of value." I would add to that sentiment, suggesting that the first person you need to believe is unique and valuable is you! That has been the focus of the work that has been done to this point, and with today's lesson you will turn the corner and begin to take your leadership out into the world.

For many people, the idea of clearly communicating their worth, value, ideas, and inspiration to others is difficult. If we fully express ourselves to others, we are lowering our defenses, and too many of us falsely believe that who we are is somehow not good enough. Leaders have confidence—first in their talents and skills, and then in their capacity to communicate what they have to offer the world in way that it is not only heard but also acted upon.

In today's society, the formula for leadership success seems to be in reverse—that is, if you are a charismatic communicator you can hide behind a persona in order to gain accolades, attention, and power, all the while knowing that your authentic self remains hidden. This path to power may take a person several rungs up the ladder, but without exception, each person who succeeds this way will have a fall from grace. Why? Because true power emanates from your authentic self and your clarity about the contribution you wish to make in the world. Only when you align your life with these principles will you be able to communicate it in a way that creates a life of leadership.

The technique to practice today is based on Marshall Rosenberg's timeless work on nonviolent communication. In your communication with others, focus on these four steps:

1. Clearly state what you observe: this should be a neutral statement that is fact-based and everyone agrees with. For example: Joe walked into the meeting ten minutes late.

2. Express how *you* feel about the observation: you need to own your feelings and express what is happening in *your* experience. For instance, you might say, "When you arrive for a meeting late, I become anxious that we won't meet our goal to end in an hour."

3. State what you need: you have the right to have your needs met, ensuring that you get what you need is important. Continuing with the example, you might say, "Joe, if you are going to be late, please let me know before the meeting so I can change the agenda, and you can speak later during the meeting."

4. Make your request: the key to effective leadership communication is to *always* ask people to do something as a result of having heard you speak. In this case, you might ask, "Would you be willing to call or text me if you are going to be late next time?"

While this is an excellent tool in communicating around differences of opinions, conflicts, and disagreement, it is also at the heart of how a leader communicates. If you can make a neutral statement about a hot topic, you are giving yourself the chance to become aware and make a choice between stimuli and response. Through the expression of *your* feelings, you are sharing your authentic self and you are open to real connection.

The statement of your needs comes from a heightened understanding of how you like to operate in the world. Your strength in making a request ensures the other person knows that you have the ability to ask for what you want—which means that you will usually get it!

From My Experience

My youngest son reminds me frequently, "Mom, you are a talker; I guess that's why you do it for a living!" Out of the mouths of babes . . . . I enjoy verbal communication and it is central to my work as a coach, teacher, and speaker, but speaking often in public and to large groups is not a requirement to be an effective leader. The key is not the amount of talking or the size of the group; the key is that each person making the Leadership Choice becomes a fluent reflection of the leader he or she already is.

Some of the most effective communicators I have known were at their best in small, intimate groups. What we ultimately remember about people we feel are effective speakers is that they share themselves in a genuine way. Lillyan Wilder, a highly regarded speech coach, called this quality "being real" in front of an audience. The beauty in this process is that effective communication comes from being comfortable with yourself, and the way to do that is to discover your authentic self. With those two building blocks, you are laying the foundation for the changes you wish to see in the world. As a bonus, you will find people responding to you in kind, opening up to you in new and more substantial ways as you open up to them. That is the leadership process: model what you wish to see in others and soon they will be following you in ways you could never have imagined!

Day *19*

Being Self-Aware in Every Moment

Photo by Michael Iskowitz

Guiding Thought for the Day

By witnessing my actions, I clearly and authentically connect with others, allowing us to move forward toward our common goals.

Repeat the thought above to yourself throughout the day as you focus on the importance of being aware of your actions in each moment. By bringing mindful awareness of your actions to your life, you ignite the process of growth and development for yourself and those around you. No one is perfect; as a leader, learning to make those adjustments each day in how you engage with others will ensure that you continue to grow, improve, and allow your expanded awareness to create greater impact on your world.

Journal Exercise

Begin your journal exercise by writing the Guiding Thought for the Day at the top of your page. Next, spend at least three minutes answering the following questions:

How often do you currently engage in self-critique? What is the goal of your critiques? What are you learning from your self-assessment? What needs to shift to allow it to be a regular and valuable part of you life?

Looking at yourself as you operate in the world isn't always easy, just as many people don't like to see themselves on video or hear an audio recording. The reason people don't enjoy these experiences is because there is a gap between how they *think* they are expressing themselves and how they are actually doing it. Self-awareness and critique gives you the ability to close that gap—to continually move toward the intention, the action, and the result you desire.

Leadership Skills: Taking Action

"We judge ourselves by what we feel capable of doing, while others judge us by what we have already done."—Henry Wadsworth Longfellow

This quote hits the proverbial nail on the head. Too often we see what we wanted to do in a situation and not what we actually did. Most people go into situations with good intentions—they want to contribute, participate, find solutions, and so forth. What gets in the way is the "humanness" that emerges as we interact with others. What if someone else looks like they have a better handle on the situation? What if your ideas aren't valued, used, or acted on? Does that person have a better style than you? The list of self-doubting questions is endless and most assuredly will crop up any time two or more people come together—especially if they are trying to achieve a goal.

In order to escape this endless cycle of questioning, you must ground yourself in the knowledge of your talents and strengths that are unchangeable—no one, no situation, nothing can take these from you as you bring your full awareness to your interactions with others. If you change the nature of the question from how others perceive you and your actions (outside in) to whether you brought the best of you to the table (inside out), you have not only shifted your focus, you have gained the power to change and improve the only thing you can—you!

The exercise for today is to shift your inner dialogue to examine *your* part of each interaction you have today. How could you have been more effective? What could you have done to change the outcome? How might you do a better job of expressing yourself? By simply changing the focus of the critique and developing a keen sense of self-awareness, you will dramatically shift your impact and thus the results of all your interactions.

From My Experience

All my life I have been an athlete, and I continue to enjoy sports and competing in my life today. For anyone who engages in these activities, competitive or not, we spend a great deal of time examining our tennis stroke, golf swing, or yoga posture. We think nothing of breaking down the tiniest element to improve our performance and achieve better results.

Today's leadership lesson is no different. If you want to be more effective and easily reach your goals, then the same level of self-awareness and self-responsibly are in order. While some may blame a coach or teammate for errors, if you shank your tee-shot or double-fault, the only person who is truly responsible is you—and the only person who can fix it is you. Leadership is no different; if you want a better performance, you need to look at what you are doing and tweak the areas that are not as effective as they could be.

Which brings me to a discussion of yoga. One of the reasons I love yoga is because it is such a great metaphor for leadership. With yoga there is a repetition of poses during each practice, and while it may seem like you are doing the same thing, each practice is somehow different. One day you may be tight in your legs, or you may be fatigued. Given your body type, some poses may easier than others, but as you practice, poses that were once challenging become easier. This is why yoga requires mindfulness.

Each day is different, and it is important to know what is needed each time to have the best possible experience.

That is the same concept I am describing with leadership awareness. Whether you are interacting with the same group of people or taking on a new challenge, the more aware you are of your participation in the process, the better able you are to create the desired outcome. As you cultivate a heightened sense of yourself, you will have greater confidence and capacity to lead anytime, anywhere.

Day 20

Creating Balanced and Productive Teams

Photo by Jason Claire

Guiding Thought for the Day

My goals are achieved by effectively working with others.

Repeat the thought above to yourself throughout the day as you focus on the importance of other people in the leadership process. Leadership implies relationship by denoting the presence of both leader and follower. While these terms have become pejorative, the essence behind the concept is that a symbiotic relationship among those with diverse skills is necessary to achieve goals. A more enlightened definition of leadership therefore allows various people at various times to step into the leadership role and for leaders to know when their skills are best utilized as a follower.

Journal Exercise

Begin your journal exercise by writing the Guiding Thought for the Day at the top of your page. Next, spend at least three minutes answering the following questions:

Describe in full detail how you typically participate in a team. What talents and skills do you like to bring? Do you allow them to be utilized in the best possible way? How can you be more effective as a leader on a team?

When talking about leadership and team, the discussion almost always moves toward how to become the person in charge, because we have been taught that if you are not in charge, you don't have any power. In today's exercise, think about the times when you and your leadership skills should not be in charge. Conversely, if you have a tendency to not step forward, are the times when your particular leadership skills are exactly what is necessary to move the team forward? Lastly, consider how the idea of leadership moving around within a team makes you feel. It may feel awkward at first, but after some reflection, it may be just the thing everyone needs.

Leadership Skills: Taking Action

"It is amazing how much you can accomplish when it doesn't matter who gets the credit."—Unknown

Making progress toward achieving a goal is an essential component of effective leadership and is the focus of today's leadership lesson. No man is an island, and no goal is accomplished alone. Teamwork is vital to success, and in order to create effective teams, each participant must play a leadership role in the process of change.

When you bring a new understanding of leadership to the group dynamic, things immediately begin to shift. People have been socialized to stake out their territory, protect their turf, and create fiefdoms of power all in the pursuit of exercising their leadership. Unfortunately, this approach only creates animosity, discomfort, and chaos amongst the group. How many examples can you think of where a noble goal was left unmet simply because the team members were unable to get past their warped understanding of leadership and created such havoc that nothing got accomplished?

By making the Leadership Choice as you begin the group process, you have made an important leadership move by offering a new paradigm for how the group works together. Through the identification of the various talents and skills at the table and the willingness to allow those with the necessary tools to lead at the appropriate time (these steps are further described in days 23–27), you have unleashed the power of the team, and the result may surprise you! Today, begin looking for ways to open up the leadership process to all those who participate and begin creating leaders of those around you.

From My Experience

Those who reach positions of leadership under the old system often find the challenge of leading in a new way difficult. This is not because those who are on the team want to keep the old power structure intact, rather it is because a personal demon says, "I made it in the old way by putting my time in and doing what it took to rise in the ranks. I had to pay the price; why not require the same thing of those I am now leading?" Hence the reason things take so long to change—if you have become part of a system that has provided you power, why should you change it?

That is why it is so important for people to begin leading in a different way now. Old habits die hard, and the longer you wait to create change, the more difficult it becomes. Learning to lead is a lifelong pursuit, and doing it in a way that will ultimately serve the greater good first and the individual as a part of that success is the only path that ensures effective leadership will take hold. Simply saying you want to lead differently but are going to do it the old way to get into a position of power won't work. Leading and being the best of who you are in every moment is the way to get there.

Day 21

Create Connections

Photo by Kathleen Schafer

Guiding Thought for the Day

Connecting with the right people at the right time allows me to easily and effortlessly achieve my goals.

Repeat this thought to yourself throughout the day as you focus on how you connect with others. To accomplish most goals, you must not only work with those on your team, you must also connect with others outside of your immediate circle of influence. Building relationships with other people allows you to bring your work fully into the world and integrate the talents and skills of others into the change process.

Journal Exercise

Begin your journal exercise by writing the Guiding Thought for the Day at the top of your page. Next, spend at least three minutes answering the following questions:

How do you connect with other people? Are you open to new connections? How do you establish rapport with others? What do you do to grow and maintain your network? Are your actions in keeping with your leadership skills and goals?

Connecting with people may seem like an everyday part of life, and my guess is that most people are not as conscious about connections as they can be. What people have crossed your path that you may have dismissed? Do you take time to cultivate the relationships you have established even if there is not immediate need or purpose? Building a broad community is essential for leaders and for effective leadership.

Leadership Skills: Taking Action

"When I help, I am aware of my strength and others' weakness . . . fixing is a form of judgment. It implies something is broken and creates a distance, a disconnection. We can only serve that which we are profoundly connected to."—Sam Daley-Harris

Being connected to the larger community around you allows a steady flow of awareness and knowledge *between* you and those you seek to serve. Connection is not a one-way street and neither is leadership. In order to be effective, it is essential that you establish, cultivate, and maintain connections with others in your community. By doing this you will create possibilities for putting your leadership into the world that cannot be planned.

Synchronistic experiences with those in your network allow for spontaneous opportunities to arise; your ability to stay open to these occurrences is what will allow your leadership to fully flourish. Examine the life of any respected leader and you find those moments when an unexpected opportunity arose and changed the life and the impact of that leader. Having the strength to stay open to and grab hold of those chances is the mark of a good leader. You never know when a life-changing event is going to happen, but being out in the world and authentically connecting to others will allow it to happen easily and often!

As you practice today's leadership lesson, be aware of the connections in your life. Who is a part of your community, and what are you doing to be an active engaged part of it? Most importantly, are you aware of the opportunities that are presenting themselves to you, and do you have the courage to follow them?

From My Experience

One experience that continually surprises my clients when they increase their awareness of their community and community involvement is how much opportunity is left on the table. Everyone is busy, people have commitments, and we are constantly electronically connected, which makes quality connections increasingly few and far between. We are always around other people, but rarely do we truly connect with them and invite them to contribute their talents and strengths.

Leaders often find themselves beleaguered by feelings of having to go it alone, of no one understanding the challenges they are facing, or not having the resources to move forward. Yet my guess is that there are myriads of people you know who have something to offer you to move you past your current hurdle. You just need to find the strength to show up, connect with others, and be open and willing to take action when the time comes. Opportunities always exist; the question is whether you are willing to identify them and then take the next step.

The other benefit that comes from authentic connection and building community is that you have the opportunity to help others and use their needs to shape your activities. Understanding the desires of the community is essential in effective leadership because offering wonderful talents and skills in a way that people can't or don't want to receive them won't help anyone. Connecting to others will always serve you well . . . and your community too!

Day 22

Managing the Pace of Change

Photo by Kathleen Schafer

Guiding Thought for the Day

Allowing change to happen at a measured pace best serves everyone and makes the journey easier.

Repeat the thought above to yourself throughout the day as you focus being relaxed about what you are creating with your leadership. In our world we become frustrated if it takes a few seconds for a Web page to load, yet the changes we seek to create within ourselves and in our communities will not happen overnight. Today your goal is to relax around the pace of change and shift your focus to enjoying the process while creating your desired outcome.

Journal Exercise

Begin your journal exercise by writing the Guiding Thought for the Day at the top of your page. Next, spend at least three minutes answering the following questions:

What fears arise in you when you don't observe things happening as fast as you would like? What is at the basis of those fears? How can you shift your perspective?

Everyone wants to see things change, grow, and expand. Leading in the change process can be challenging because the first steps are often invisible. Just like the story about checking on the growing carrots by pulling them up too soon, we often get frustrated if we don't see immediate results and in that frustration prolong or damage the outcome. Today's exercise asks you to examine that impatience and develop strategies for enjoying the process.

Leadership Skills: Taking Action

"It is always the simple things that change our lives. And these things never happen when you are looking for them to happen. Life will reveal answers at the pace life wishes to do so. You feel like running, but life is on a stroll."—Donald Miller

"To climb steep hills requires slow pace at first."—William Shakespeare

Change is the only constant in life, and it is the thing we wrestle with all the time! Too much, not enough, too slow, too fast, wrong time, or wrong way—whatever it is that we wish to see happen often occurs in a different way. Learning to effectively manage the pace of change for yourself and those around you is an important component of effective leadership. The irony of this leadership skill is that it is the one over which you have the least control, so the key is to learn to work *with* the tides of change to create your desired result.

The best example I have for working with change is to think about it like the seasons of the year. Spring, summer, fall, and winter each bring a change of weather, activity, and opportunities to do different things, and no two years will be exactly alike. Just like a farmer who pays close attention to minute changes in the weather and then adjusts when to sow his seeds or harvest his crops accordingly, so too must a leader understand the environment in which he or she is attempting to sow seeds of change to produce the best harvest.

A farmer knows that he cannot control the weather and the same is true for a leader. There are too many factors that you *can't* control—the key is to stay alert and receptive to the changing environment and use your best judgment as to when to move ahead and when to let the ground lie fallow. For today, look at your life and let go of things of that you can't control. Allow yourself to be attuned to making the best decisions you can make for yourself and others in this moment. By increasing your awareness of and action about what you can control, you will be able to ride out the waves of change with ease and grace.

From My Experience

Of all the leadership skills I work with, this is the one that is most personally challenging. When I set my mind to something, I want it to happen *now*! And for years, I created aggravation for others and myself by not discerning the things that I can control and those I can't. As with many things, age and experience have combined to allow me to understand that if I am agitated while working through the change process, even if I achieve my goal, I have robbed myself of the value and beauty of the experience.

People often recognize this tendency in themselves when it comes to their childhood or their children. In both cases, people frequently find themselves wishing something would be different (e.g., "When I am older, I can...," or "Once she is potty-trained it will be so..."). Whatever the desired change, it is fascinating how often people look back at lost opportunities to see truly what they were experiencing in that moment. Leadership becomes the chance to establish the direction in which you are moving while still appreciating what is happening on the way there.

If you can fully embrace the capacity to create change and the patience to allow it to unfold at its own pace, you have truly achieved success. For me, this is a quality I continue to cultivate in my own life—one I will likely never fully master, yet I endeavor to enjoy the process of creating in my life and work.

Day 23

Creating Buy-in

Photo by Karin Heinzl

Guiding Thought for the Day

Allowing others to join me through their own inspiration is the greatest leadership achievement.

As you think about today's lesson, repeat the thought above to yourself throughout the day. Focus on the important leadership quality that inspires others to join you by making the choice for themselves. Too often leadership implies that those who are following have no choice and don't get to exercise their individuality. True leadership means that all those on the team choose to be there and bring their best to the group effort.

Journal Exercise

Begin your journal exercise by writing the Guiding Thought for the Day at the top of your page. Next, spend at least three minutes answering the following questions:

Why is it important for everyone to have choice about his or her participation in the team? How can you reinforce their ownership in the process? How will this dynamic impact the final results?

We all know that "buy-in" is important for a healthy team, and the way in which this usually happens is everyone gathers together and the leader explains what will happen and then asks everyone if it is okay. That isn't buy-in. Buy-in happens when people choose to be a part of the group because they are inspired by the mission and by their role within the group. Based on leadership style, it will vary for each person and each group, but the core principle remains the same—to lead effective teams, inspire those around you, and allow them to come to you and join your work.

Leadership Skills: Taking Action

"The best of leaders when the job is done, when the task is accomplished, the people will say we have done it ourselves."—Lao Tzu

"If your actions inspire others to dream more, learn more, do more and become more, you are a leader."—John Quincy Adams

As we begin our understanding of the importance of team building, the first step is to learn how people get to the table. No one enjoys the feeling that they "have" to do something; everyone wants to enjoy their work and feel that they are contributing to something great. If there is no sense of cohesion, then barriers go up, connections are lost, and the product of such efforts are stilted. This seems logical, and still millions of people go to work in groups, teams, offices, and organizations where dynamics like this play themselves out multiple times daily. Living the Leadership Choice means creating teams in a different way, and you must allow people to come to you.

People always point out that more often than not they *can't* choose whether to participate on a team or not—it is dictated by someone else, usually an authority figure. As a leader, you understand that you do have a choice in every situation. Your choice may be that have elected to work for a particular company, and by doing so you will work with people that have a different leadership mindset than you would like. Nonetheless, you made a choice to be there—so make the best of it. By simply shifting your perspective from feeling as if you *have* to do it to understanding that it is your choice, you have dramatically shifted the dynamics of your participation and how you will interact with the rest of the group, which will ultimately shift them as well.

As a leader of a group effort, you have the responsibility to inspire others by modeling the opportunity of choice in all you do. If you unleash the leadership potential and inspiration of your team members, you can be assured of a positive outcome. Being able to see your team's potential helps them to see it as well. Less directing and more unearthing are fundamental—use your talents to open up the possibilities and allow everyone to chose the *best* contribution they can make. Now you have created an energy that will move the group forward with ease—and much less effort from you!

From My Experience

People often become scared when leading teams because they feel that they must always remain in control. But as we have discussed, controlling all facets of your surroundings is impossible. The benefit of creating team buy-in is that everyone assumes responsibility for what takes places and it doesn't fall on the shoulders of one person. If everyone on the team understands their part and their responsibility for making it happen, then each person bears the weight and the opportunity equally with the leader.

In a team with full buy-in from each of its members, blame falls away as individuals understand that they have the responsibility for the outcome and become personally invested in ensuring it is as good as it can possibly be. It is fun to be a part of such a team because camaraderie and mutual support blossom.

On teams like this, the role of leader becomes less visible and the contribution of the team and its results become the focus. Sure one person doesn't get all the credit and the goal is generally accomplished beyond the expectations of all involved.

Day 24

Engaging Everyone's Talents and Skills

Photo by Kathleen Schafer

Guiding Thought for the Day

All things are possible when each person's talents are contributed and used in the best possible way.

As you think about today's lesson, repeat this thought to yourself. Focus on the importance of various people's talents and skills. To meet your goals, there are people who have something to offer that either you don't want to do or don't have the natural inclination to do. By valuing and including each set of talents, you will be able to reach your goals easily and effectively.

111

Journal Exercise

Begin your journal exercise by writing the Guiding Thought for the Day at the top of your page. Next, spend at least three minutes answering the following questions:

Are you able to identify the talents and skills of others? Do you effectively integrate those talents into the group effort? What keeps you from allowing other team members to give the best they have to offer? What can you do to change this dynamic?

Most of us understand that everyone has their strengths. For instance, when one person is very detail-oriented, that usually means that he or she is not as adept at seeing the big picture, and vice versa. Yet too many people constantly feel pressure to be all things to all people, especially in group dynamics. Today's exercise is to examine your role in keeping the competition alive and to reflect on how to create different outcomes by using complimentary skills *together* in achieving team goals.

Leadership Skills: Taking Action

"None of us is as smart as all of us."—Ken Blanchard

"No one can whistle a symphony. It takes a whole orchestra to play it."—H. E. Luccock

The idea of a symphony is a good comparison to leadership. Each musician is a master of his instrument and is someone who knows how to make it sing in a way no other person can. Each instrument is important, and yet they are different. What allows them to come together in a harmonious way is the conductor or leader. She is the person who coordinates all the others, allowing them to bring their best skills to the performance, queuing them when it's time to come forward, signaling when it is time to step back, and at the right moment unleashing the talent of the entire group to move forward to the completion of their goal. Each person in the orchestra needs the others to perform the piece, and the leader doesn't play an instrument at all—she creates the opportunity for each part to contribute at the right time, in the right way, to reach an outcome they are all proud of.

When leadership becomes about unleashing the talents of others, your energy is freed to focus on the forward motion of the whole while each member enthusiastically plays their parts. To provide a framework for the ways in which groups work together, I created the Cycle of Change, which outlines the four main leadership intelligences and how the work together to create changes. Any one of the types can be the leader; it is simply up to each person to know where his or her skills lie and for the leader to call them forth at the right time.

Cycle of Change:

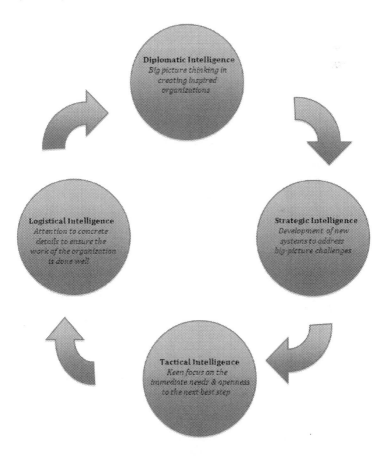

- Initiation of Change with the Diplomatic Intelligence

  These people are able to discern long-range issues and trends ahead of the crowd and connect people to the importance of addressing these issues through their passions and feelings. Because they are compelling, Diplomats bring people to the table to begin developing solutions.

- Development of Strategy with the Strategic Intelligence

  These individuals love to develop solutions to new challenges and work to improve existing systems. They are strong, intelligent people who think outside the box to create innovative approaches to problems, and most enjoy the formulation and not implementation of their plans.

- Grounding the Strategy with the Tactical Intelligence

  Once a problem has been identified and a strategy developed, it is important to make it work on the ground. Those with tactical intelligence love to figure out the appropriate steps to take to reach the goal and are open to moving forward in the best way given the reality of the moment.

- Working the Strategy with the Logistical Intelligence

  As the tacticians devise the steps to take, it is up to the Logicians to make things happen. These "engines of society" are the gurus of what it takes to move step-by-step toward the goal. They are detail-oriented people who keep the team organized, on time, and on budget.

While there is greater depth to this model, you can see how each person has an important role to play at various stages in the process of change. As you move through your day today, notice which one of these roles is your strength and see if you can identify others' strengths. (A hint: these correspond to Keirsey's Temperament Types discussed in Day Four.) Then as you look at your team, see if you can dertermine how and why your team functions based on the talents and strengths of its members and if they are currently being used in the best possible way.

From My Experience

Working with this model has proven to be one of the most effective things I have seen in team development for two important reasons. First, it allows everyone to experience a big sigh of relief as they understand that they get to do what they most enjoy and others get to do the same, which means trying to be all things to all people gets pushed to the wayside. Second, teams work better when the people with the right skills are doing the right job!

How many times have you been a part of a team that was constantly hindered by people trying to do things they simply weren't good at? And while everyone gets it, too often people are afraid to acknowledge where their skills are and where they end. The beauty in this model is that everyone has an important role to play and they are different—no better, no worse—than others. By staying true to your authentic self, you are free to say, "This is not my strength" and to allow others to shine in their authentic way. It doesn't mean you lose control; in fact, quite the opposite. You gain control because now people are not talking about what you can't do, they are focused on your power to allow others to be all they can be!

Day 25

Using Conflict as a Tool for Growth

Photo by Michael Iskowitz

Guiding Thought for the Day

Conflict means people care, and when I connect to the passion in each person it shows me the way forward.

Repeat the thought above to yourself throughout the day as you focus on the opportunity that conflict presents for growth. While not always fun, understanding how to successfully resolve issues by creating new paths to move forward is the hallmark of effective leadership.

Journal Exercise

Begin your journal exercise by writing the Guiding Thought for the Day at the top of your page. Next, spend at least three minutes answering the following questions in your own hand.

How do you feel about conflict? How do you handle it? Identify three things that you can do differently the next time you encounter it.

Even bringing up the idea of conflict makes most people uncomfortable, and for those who relish a good fight, they frequently use conflict as a way *not* to deal authentically with others and develop effective solutions. Conflict is a part of life that will not change; learning how you can use these moments as opportunities to grow and move forward is one of the most important leadership lessons you can master.

Leadership Skills: Taking Action

"Conflict is the beginning of consciousness."—M. Esther Harding

"Whenever you're in conflict with someone, there is one factor that can make the difference between damaging the relationship and deepening it. That factor is attitude."—William James

When people talk about conflict it generally insinuates not just a disagreement, but one that is protracted, messy, ugly, and uncomfortable—and who wants that in their life. Still, people have learned to live with various conflicts in their lives because they lack the tools to effectively address issues with people who feel strongly about a certain topic. If you learn nothing else about leadership, learning to effectively deal with conflict is the one tool that will serve you well time and again.

Here is the Leadership Connection model for conflict resolution:

- For you:
  - Identify what you are feeling. This means separating the facts—i.e., the things that all parties can agree on—from your feelings.

- o Identify the true root issue for you. In almost every situation it has to do with fear. You may want to frame your response this way: "My fear in this conflict is that if *blank* happens it will mean *blank* for me."
- o Examine your root concern. Is what you are thinking, feeling, or fearing absolutely true? Have you perhaps allowed emotions and thoughts to make the consequences larger than they really are?
- o What is the desired outcome you would like to see? Be clear about what you would like to happen and how you want the conflict to be resolved.

- For the other person or party involved in the conflict:

  Go through these exact same steps *from their point of view.* This may be difficult, but the process of looking at the situation from the other person's perspective will give you new insights into how to effectively move forward.

- Meet with the other person/people involved

  While meeting face-to-face can be uncomfortable, the power of this experience is what is needed to resolve it. In extending the invitation to sit down, be clear about your intention to resolve the issue at hand. When meeting, work through the conversation using the nonviolent communication method discussed on Day 18. In addition to making specific requests aimed at breaking the logjam, your empathy will be heightened by having engaged in the first two steps of this process. Just as a high-functioning team leader identifies the talents of others, you can use these same insights to help the other party identify his or her fears and address possible resolutions that he or she may not considered.

I assure you that if you engage in this process, you will be several steps down the road toward resolving whatever issue is before you. The other party has a choice as to how he or she is going to handle it, and if he or she wants to work toward a good-faith resolution. In the very worst case, the other person will be completely unwilling or unable to engage at this level—and then you will *know* that you have done all you can to resolve the issue. Once you know this, you can make more informed choices about how you want to move forward. Regardless, you win by either resolving the conflict and strengthening the connection or knowing that the conflict cannot currently be resolved. Now you can confidentially chose a new direction knowing that you have done your best in the current situation.

From My Experience

Conflict is never fun, but that doesn't mean that it is not beneficial and useful. You have so much to offer as a leader that spending inordinate amounts of time on energy-draining issues is the last thing that you want to do. Learning how to tackle conflicts head-on in a timely way keeps them from festering and draining you and your team of energy.

Sometime it takes us a while to understand that we are in conflict with someone, but once that becomes clear, it is important to engage in this process. Life is too short to occupy your mind occupied with someone else's baggage—leadership is about the freedom and empowerment of the authentic self, and if that is your sincere intention, conflict becomes rare. When it does arise, it is because fear has taken over. Just remember that you can only control your piece of the situation and the other person is responsible for his or her piece. You cannot fix or change anyone. The best you can do is offer to work things through and then do it. If you are not matched in the process, you have a choice to do different things in different ways and in different places. Regardless of the outcome, you have stayed true to yourself and connected to your power.

Day 26

Allowing Individuals and the Team to Grow

Photo by Karin Heinzl

Guiding Thought for the Day

As we grow, we change, and allowing growth and welcoming change keeps teams vital.

Repeat the thought above to yourself throughout the day as you focus on surrendering to the only constant in life—change! Teams rely on a healthy dynamic among their members, and the way to maintain that is to accept growth and change as a natural part of the group experience.

Journal Exercise

Begin your journal exercise by writing the Guiding Thought for the Day at the top of your page. Next, spend at least three minutes answering the following questions in your own hand.

How do you ensure lifelong growth for yourself? For your team?

Some people enjoy change perhaps a bit too much while others find change difficult to accept. Today's exercise is to make peace with your relationship with change and find a healthy balance so that you and your team continue to function as you move through it. Now that you are beginning to understand your current relationship with change, answer this question: *In the ideal, how would you like to handle all future changes in your life? List three things that you will endeavor to do as new opportunities for growth come into your life.*

Leadership Skills: Taking Action

"Think of managing change as an adventure. It tests your skills and abilities. It brings forth talent that may have been dormant. Change is also a training ground for leadership. When we think of leaders, we remember times of change, innovation and conflict. Leadership is often about shaping a new way of life. To do that, you must advance change, take risks and accept responsibility for making change happen."—Charles E. Rice

If you are like many people, you have been taught to believe that success is reaching a goal and working like crazy to keep what you accomplished. After all, once you have things where you want them, it is natural to want to keep them the same way. Alas, life doesn't work that way, and neither do effective teams. As a team moves through challenges and develops new competencies, the individuals on the team experience the same phenomenon and with that growth comes the choice—change for the better or change for worse. As a leader, you can support your team members in choosing change that expands growth and opportunities for everyone.

Keeping team members engaged and excited about the process of change stems not only from an awareness of it nature and reality; you must provide a roadmap as well. This course helps people walk through the change process and allows them to grow and cultivate their leadership talents and skills so that they can put their best into the world. It is not a process you go through once and are done. After you or your team members have achieved goals, it is time to revisit the steps again. How have your talents and skills evolved? What new changes are you interested in making? Is your life still aligned? While you may not need to spend as much time in every area as you did the first time through, continuing to revisit this material as your life spirals up will provide you and your team with fresh insights on how to grow and create what you want in your life and with your work.

The same is true for your team. As you prepare to enter new phases and challenges, review the contributions of team members. How has the work evolved? Are the right people still in the right places? Are there some people who need to go? Others who need to be added? By approaching growth and change within a team as an opportunity to keep it healthy, people moving in, out, and around becomes commonplace and doesn't create havoc and hurt feelings.

Today, take a moment to look at the team with which you are involved. How is growth supported? How does the team grow and create new opportunities for itself and its members?

From My Experience

Change . . . sometimes I love it, other times I hate it, but as I have evolved as a leader, I have learned to accept it as necessary for growth. Our humanity creates in us a longing to develop our talents, to create new experiences, and make greater contributions in our world. The expansion of our horizons is vital to our leadership and our happiness.

As individuals it is often easy to see how growth is positive for us. When it comes to teams the dynamic is much different, and people can sometimes become hesitant about suggesting or making changes. As you accept the flow of growth as natural, teams too can benefit from the ebb and flow. Making teams work means constantly managing the pace of change—and that is best handled by accepting growth as a positive outcome of success.

Day 27

Knowing When I Am Done and It Is Time to Move On

Photo by Karin Heinzl

Guiding Thought for the Day

All things must come to an end, and in that ending lies the promise of brilliant new beginnings.

Repeat this thought to yourself as you focus on the idea that life and leadership are full of endings and beginning and both contain the seeds of the other. We are socialized to believe that beginnings are good and endings bad, and this belief often keeps us from fully embracing this powerful dynamic. Both experiences are facts of life and essential for our growth and development.

Journal Exercise

Begin your journal exercise by writing the Guiding Thought for the Day at the top of your page. Next, spend at least three minutes answering the following questions:

How do you feel about beginnings? Endings? How have these feelings impacted how you handled a leadership situation? What needs to shift in you to allow these experiences to flow easily in and out of your life?

As you begin thinking about your answers, my guess is that you will find that you enjoy one of these phenomena much more than the other. You will likely see that during one of these experiences you internalized that it was bad or unpleasant. Think about how that experience is shaping your behavior today. How are those beliefs keeping you from fully opening up to all that beginnings and endings have to offer? As a leader, if you can fully embrace this flow of initiation and completion, you will have mastered one of life's greatest challenges and tapped into a power you never knew existed.

Leadership Skills: Taking Action

"Every new beginning comes from some other beginning's end."—Senaca

"What we call the beginning is often the end. And to make an end is to make a beginning. The end is where we start from."—T. S. Eliot

Grabbing hold of a vision, building a team, developing a strategy, and putting it into practice are often the exciting parts of leadership work because we believe that creating is the essence of our value. It's equally important for leadership success to recognize when the time comes to end your current work and how to step out gracefully. Every person and every team will run its course, and the key to a successful beginning of the next endeavor is to understand when to step back and allow others to bring their creative energy to a new beginning.

Sometimes it is an individual who needs to move one; other times the team needs to recognize that its work in a particular endeavor has reached its finale. How do you know when it is time to move on? The following questions provide a framework for making the decision either as an individual or as a team:

The Beginning/Ending Evaluator

- **What is the current status of your authentic self?** How have your talents and skills grown? Are they still the best fit for the achievement of the goal?

- **Are you still passionate about the change you are creating?**

- **Is your life in alignment with your work and goals?** Are you able to continue along this path and keep your life in alignment?

- **Are you using and growing your leadership skills in the best possible way?** Is there room to continue evolving your leadership in this situation?

- **Is the team vital and high functioning?** Is your role within the team critical to its success? Are you able to provide your highest and best leadership? Does the team agree with your assessment?

- **Are you achieving real-world results?** What was the original goal? Has that goal been achieved? If not, has significant progress been made? Have you determined that the goal is not achievable at this moment and established a new goal?

If you answered yes to these questions, then you are likely still on the right path. If you answered no to any of these, it is time for you to reflect on your current path and have some open and honest conversations with your team. There is no right or wrong answer—by honestly answering these questions, the outcome should allow you and your team to move forward in best possible way.

From My Experience

The person I use as the greatest example of one who knew when to leave is one of America's greatest leaders—the first president of the United States, George Washington. During his storied career, he stepped away from his leadership role *four times*. Each time he knew there was something that needed to shift, and his willingness to walk away from his position of power because it was the right thing to do was one of the main reasons he was repeatedly asked to take on positions of ever-increasing importance. He demonstrated through his actions that he was keenly aware of this powerful leadership skill.

Moving on to new challenges that are in sync with the person you are becoming will serve you well throughout your life. While this is not an invitation to head for the hills when the going gets tough, it is an opening for you to regularly examine whether your current role continues to be the best fit for you and your team. So many issues arise because people tend to stay in places or situations simply because of inertia. It takes some major life circumstance to force them to make a change. Leaders get ahead of the curve and choose to make a transition before life does it for them.

Day 28

Creating Real World Results

Photo by Kathleen Schafer

Guiding Thought for the Day

As I live the Leadership Choice each day, I create real-world results.

Repeat the thought above to yourself throughout the day as you celebrate the process you will complete today. Congratulations! By choosing to take this course, you have and will continue to experience great shifts in your impact on the world and in your day-to-day happiness and satisfaction with your life.

Journal Exercise

Begin your journal exercise by writing the Guiding Thought for the Day at the top of your page. Next, spend at least three minutes answering the following questions:

How does it feel to create real-world results? What will it feel like to achieve your goals and desired change that you identified earlier in the course?

Envisioning what the end product looks like is important for anyone seeking to achieve his or her vision. Knowing what it will feel like when you accomplish a goal is the secret ingredient. The more leaders feel their actions and goals from a place of knowing what they will manifest, the quicker and easier it will become a reality.

Leadership Skills: Taking Action

"In matters of style, swim with the current; in matters of principle, stand like a rock."—Thomas Jefferson

"People who produce good results feel good about themselves."—Ken Blanchard

As you reflect on your accomplishment and growth during this course, the goal from this point forward is to fully live your leadership in the world. As these two quotes suggest, the way in which you do it may change with the times, but if you stay true to your core principles and your authentic self, you will achieve results you can't even imagine right now while feeling great along the way!

Today's leadership action is all about holding the vision of your leadership and your goals as achieved in your mind's eye as you go about your day. Think about all you can achieve with your newfound understandings, talents, and insights. Feel what it will be like when you fully exercise your leadership talents, and revel in the positive emotions it creates in you and the others around you.

Tonight, after you have spent your day fully embodying your leadership potential—return to your journal and write down what you experienced. Take note of the positive energy, emotions, stamina, and strength that you have as a result of focusing on the possibilities and not the problems—and then resolve to do the same thing each day until it becomes second nature to you. I assure you there is no faster or easier way to real world results than this process.

From My Experience

Whenever we decide to try something new, we begin to change *our* world. When you seek to exercise your leadership in service to your community, you begin to change *the* world. By doing both, you create the possibilities of great personal happiness and satisfaction along with the joy that comes from making a lasting and sustained contribution to humankind. Nothing is better than creating a life of wholeness by bringing the two together.

That is the lesson I wish to leave with you at the completion of this course; for leaders to be truly effective, one is not possible without the other. You must care as passionately for your own joy, happiness, and peace of mind as you do for others—and if you cultivate both with equal vigor, you will be successful beyond your wildest expectations. If you fail to act on both fronts, challenges will abound because it is no longer possible to effectively do one thing and say another. Just look at the institutions crumbling around us led by individuals who are not committed to the greater good.

The flip side is that great service no longer requires great sacrifice—you can be an amazing leader and live the life you want to live. Wholeness is the answer, balance is the way, and leadership is how it is done!

Part III

The Journey Continues

Chapter 3

The Real-World Results
You Can Expect to Achieve

After completing the twenty-eight days, two questions are likely swirling in your mind: what can I expect to be different, and what's next? In this chapter I discuss the expected results you will see in your life as you continue to practice your leadership skills, and in the last chapter, I offer suggestions on how you can continue to incorporate these lessons throughout your life. Regardless of where you were when you started the course, if you have sincerely endeavored in your daily exercises, I am certain that you feel very different today that you did just one month ago.

If there is one thing in my life that has caused upset and frustration, it is the *timing* associated with change. As I discussed on Day 22, learning to flow with the pace of change is fundamental and crucial for you as you move to the next stage. For most, finishing the course means that there has been a great deal of internal shifting; that is, how you are feeling about yourself, what you want to do, and how you want to do it. After just one month, the external reflection of those changes may be quite minimal. You must continue to focus on the work you have done beneath the surface and believe that over time, you will begin to experience changes in your external world.

Feeling better about yourself and your leadership skills is an important first step. As you move forward from this course, here are some of the external shifts you will start to observe in your life and work:

- *Greater Ease and Enjoyment.* The better you feel about yourself, the more you are anchored in your talents, skills, and abilities, and the greater clarity you bring about your desired contribution to the world, the lighter and easier life becomes. While even a grain of sand is irritating as it rubs against your skin, you have now cleared away much of the debris that was keeping your leadership potential from effortlessly shining forth. Situations where you feel unempowered, questions about your direction and worth, and lack of clarity about right action should be less prevalent. You have developed numerous resources to effectively address issues as they arise and your overall satisfaction with your life will increase as you stay focused on Living the Leadership Choice.

- *Understanding Where Your Efforts Will Have the Greatest Impact.* We all know that there are many things that we *can* do and often do relatively well. Each one of us yearns to find that thing that no one can do quite like us. After completing the course, you should have a much better sense of the path that will lead you to your life's purpose. As with any experience, finding your purpose is not a finite experience—it will continue to grow, shift, and change as your life does. The important lesson to remember is that by continuing to Live the Leadership Choice, you will ensure that you are marrying your leadership skills and your work in the best possible way for your life as it is right now. As you achieve that delicate balance today, you open up a world of possibilities for how that may shift for you in the future.

A great example of this phenomenon is Oprah Winfrey. For decades she has followed her talents and passion, all the while continuing to evolve in her work and the contributions she makes each day. From local talk show host to syndicated daytime star to magazine editor to creator of a television network, she has consistently followed her passion and desire to contribute to the world in a way that supports her growth and evolution as a leader. At different times in her life, her leadership looks different, but the consistent theme is she always endeavors to put her best self forward in the moment.

- *Faster Response Times to Changing Circumstances.* Change is all around us in every moment, and one reason so many people find that disconcerting is that they are not anchored within themselves. After completing the twenty-eight days, you are likely experiencing a deep connection to yourself, your leadership skills and those qualities about yourself that do not change. Having created this firm ground, you will find that you are able to quickly and effectively deal with a variety of circumstances because *you* are already clear about who you are and what you are about. Most people don't like change because it causes them to rethink or reevaluate themselves from a perspective outside of themselves. By thoroughly cultivating your authentic self and confidently walking it in the world, you bring confidence, calmness, and assuredness to changing situations, which allows you to effectively move through experiences without taking on the chaos. This skill will attract the attention of others as they seek to better their own capacity to deal with rapid change.

- *Deeper Communication and Greater Buy-in among Teammates*: Throughout the course I have discussed the power of one to impact many. As you Live the Leadership Choice, you will find those with whom you are living and working changing as you do. As you consciously choose to live authentically, communicate clearly who you are, and align your life with your passion, others will respond to you differently because you are different. Your choice to deepen your sense of self and purpose will naturally lead to greater connection with those around you, both in terms of the quality of your interactions and the impact your interactions have on achieving your goals.

- *Capacity to Create Lasting Change.* While change is something that remains constant in our lives, it is possible to move ourselves, and inspire others, to higher and more satisfactory levels of existence. Some decades ago, people didn't consider seatbelts in cars to be essential in saving lives; today few of us think twice about putting one on before starting a car. Eating better, caring for the environment, human rights—these are only a few examples of shifts that have taken place because leaders felt that purpose strongly within themselves and took action to put it out into the world. You too will experience those shifts as you commit to Living the Leadership Choice. Each day look for the incremental changes in your life and commend yourself on how you are progressing toward your goals. Be grateful for the knowledge and awareness that you have acquired that allows you see your life in an entirely new way. The more gratitude and excitement that you feel during the process, the faster, easier, and more fun it will be. The goal is not simply for you to put your leadership into the world; it is for you to have fun, enjoy it, and be expansively happy in all that you do. Now that you know what results to expect, you will start to see them in all kinds of new and interesting places.

Chapter 4

Reflect and Refocus

As you come to the end of this endeavor, it is important to celebrate your accomplishment. We are programmed to keep moving toward the next summit, so we often fail to take the time to enjoy the view from the plateau we have just reached. By completing these twenty-eight days, you have accomplished something very few have—you have *acted* on your sincere desire to live *your* life in the best possible way. Every person alive has felt the desire to live life differently, but you have actually taken steps to own your ability to change your life and the world in which we live. Congratulations!

Before taking another step, do something wonderful for yourself. Treat yourself to something that signifies the value you place on your happiness and acknowledges that each day you will continue along the path more conscious of the possibilities before you. We rarely treat ourselves the way we wish others would treat us; go ahead and do something wonderful for you. By giving yourself this gift, it will be easier for others to do it as well.

After you have completed the course and celebrated your accomplishment, what comes next? For each person, the answer to this question will be different. Listed below are some of the most common ways to move forward in Living the Leadership Choice.

Restart the Course

Many people find that the lessons and experiences this course contains are so full of information that it is difficult to take it all in at once. By revisiting the course you will likely find new insights as you become aware of how you have changed since taking it the first time. People generally need to hear something five to seven times before it becomes internalized in their thinking. Repeating the course is not about going back to do it again. It is about the opportunity to ground these concepts in your daily activities so that it is no long something you are consciously aware of but rather a natural part of your life.

Revisit Areas of Particular Interest or Resistance

The course is divided into the various stages of the Leadership Model of Change. Depending on what is going on in your life, there may be areas of the model that are particularly relevant to what you are experiencing. In general, people usually find themselves extremely interested in one area because it directly speaks to a current need in their lives. By going back through these lessons, you can put them to use in your immediate situation. It's also very common for people to find one area extremely difficult and uncomfortable to get through. If that has been your experience, it is likely because there are deep, profound lessons for you in these areas and some fear has surfaced because of this. Using the Emotional Release Technique discussed on Day 16, work to identify and release the fears about that particular leadership lesson. Once you have completed that, you can return to the material with fresh eyes and new outlook on the potential to put the lesson to work in your life.

Create a Reference Tool for Living the Leadership Choice

Just as each of us has certain natural talents and strengths, there will be certain parts of the course that come naturally and others that will require ongoing attention. Note those areas in which you need support or that you find particularly helpful when you are dealing with stressful situations so that you can quickly and easily return to them. You may want to begin a practice of reviewing key parts of the course weekly, bi-weekly, or monthly to ensure that you are staying on track in your leadership.

Life is a journey—and so too is *Living the Leadership Choice*. There is no end point, no single goal to reach. Keeping the lessons in this course fresh will ensure that you have a resource to turn to when you feel uncertain about the next step. There is no going back with this work; each time you return to these lessons you will be in a different place, and the lessons will create different responses in you. By staying present in your work, you will see that you are not returning to the same place, but rather to a familiar one that you will view with fresh eyes. With that wonder and excitement, Living the Leadership Choice will be a rewarding experience for you and for everyone touched by your life.

Final Thoughts from Kathleen

The experience of writing this book has been a leadership journey of its own—and one I am more fully appreciating all the time. It is my sincere desire that everyone who chooses to Live the Leadership Choice creates a life that they only thought possible in their dreams and a world that supports that for everyone. Each of us has a unique contribution to make, and this book is a part of mine.

I hope that the lessons contained in this book remain timeless and relevant to your life and work. Having books that I can turn to when in need, doubt, or uncertainty has been a saving grace for me. Knowing that someone has highlighted, underlined, bookmarked, and saved pieces of the work that have spoken deeply to him or her is the best compliment I can receive—for it is my passion to support as many people as possible in being the best leader they can be.

Best wishes for your journey, and my heartfelt and sincere gratitude for choosing it—the world wants what you have to offer, and now is the time for you to begin giving it.

Acknowledgments

As discussed in this book, no one accomplishes anything without the contribution of others. We embark on our journey to understand and accept ourselves alone, but in order to bring our gifts into full physical manifestation, we must work with others who will share their gifts in support of our goals. This book is the culmination of more than twenty years devoted to learning about leadership, leaders, people, and what it takes to make our world a better place.

Throughout my journey, so many people have touched my life, altered my course, and contributed to me becoming the person I am today that I could not begin to acknowledge them all here. Those I mention below have had a direct impact on bringing this book to fruition, and their support has been invaluable to the creative process. Thank you to everyone who has played a part—your life, your leadership, and your actions are a part of this accomplishment.

- Bill Savage, who first saw my love of leadership and encouraged me to pursue it.

- Chris Arterton, who saw in me talents and strengths I had yet to own and gave me the opportunity to develop them.

- Cathy Allen, who provided me a model for feminine leadership and an understanding of the necessity of bringing it to our policy-making bodies.

- Ina Gjikondi, whose passion for leadership and service to others has created a bond in this work that is integral to its success.

- Rana Sweiss, whose passion for changing the inequities in the Middle East helped shaped these concepts to apply equally to all.

- Karin Heinzl, who loved this work and encouraged creating a course so that people throughout the world could access this work anytime, anywhere.

- Chris Bell, who saw the power and potential of this work long before others and contributed the concept of "The Leadership Choice."

- Susan Henkels, who read the first draft of this book and whose feedback provided me with the confidence to move forward in this process with joy.

- Marla Wald, my dear friend who has always been there for me when I needed someone most.

- Kenna Akash, who loved me enough to help me see the power of creativity in transforming my life.

- Michael Iskowitz, who kept on loving me, no matter what

Lastly, to my students, clients, and audiences—your courage to share your leadership pursuits with me allowed the insights in this book to be developed and serve others, which is the true meaning of leadership.

References

Larry Copeland. "Americans Give Thumbs up to Free Time—Mostly TV," *usatoday.com* McClean, VA: USA Today, December 23, 2010.

David J. Ekerdt and Bosse R. "*Change in Self-Reported Health with Retirement*," The International Journal of Aging and Human Development, Volume 15, Number 3, PP. 213–23. Amityville, NY: Baywood Publishing Company.

"Self-Esteem Drops after Retirement," *LifeScience.com*, New York, TechMedia Network, April 1, 2010.

"As Benefits Costs Rise, Employee Retirement Savings Decline," *ameriprise. com*, November 13, 2006.

Molly Moore. "*Virgina Killings Widely Seen as Reflecting a Violent Society; World Reaction Mixes Condolences with Critism of Policies.*" The Washington Post Foreign Service, April 18, 2007.

Henry A. Kissinger. "*Lee Kuan Yew: Singapore's Master Strategist.*" Time Magazine, May 10, 2010.

Interview with Vice President Dick Cheney, NBC, "Meet the Press." Transcript for March 16, 2003.

Carl Gustav Jung. 1875–1961. Swiss psychiatrist, psychologist, and founder of analytic psychology. www.ThinkExist.com.

Erma Bombeck. 1927–1996. US writer and humorist. www.ThinkExist.com.

Don Richard Riso. Understanding the Enneagram. Boston: Houghton Mifflin Company (2000).

John Maxwell. American author and motivational speaker. www.ThinkExist.com.

Zhuge Liang (181–234), Chinese military strategist, statesman, scholar and inventor. www.civicsusa.com

Thomas J. Watson (1874–1956). American entrepreneur and founder of IBM. www.brainyquote.com.

James Belasco and Stayer, R. Flight of the Buffalo (1994), www.leadershipnow.com

Margaret Mead. 1901–1978. www.thinkexist.com.

Lance Secretan. Industry Week. October 12, 1998. www.theleadershiphub.com

Paul Hawken. Environmentalist and entrepreneur. www.ThinkExist.com.

Thich Nhat Hanh. Vietnamese zen master. www.scholars.umd.edu/serviceday/quotes.pdf

Albert Camus. Philosopher and writer. www.scholars.umd.edu/serviceday/quotes.pdf

Anais Nin (1903–1977). Author. www.quotationspage.com

Zig Ziglar. Motivational speaker. www.planetmotivation.com

Anwar Sadat (1970–1981). President of Egypt. www.thinkexist.com

Ronald Heifetz.. Leadership Without Easy Answers, Harvard University Press, 1994.

Earl Nightingale (1921–1989). Motivational writer and speaker. www.thinkexist.com

Frank Gaines. www.quotationsbook.com

James Humes. www.leadershipnow.com

Henry Wadsworth Longfellow. www.brainyquote.com

Daley-Harris. www.scholars.umd.edu/serviceday/quotes.pdf

Marshall Rosenberg. www.cnvc.org

Donald Miller. www.thinkexist.com

William Shakespeare. (1564–1616). www.Thinkexist.com

Lao Tzu. www.inspringquotes4u.blogspot.com.

John Quincy Adams (1767–1848). www.Thinkexist.com

Ken Blanchard. www.values.com

H. E. Luccock. www.quotes4u.blogspot.com

M. Esther Harding. www.Thinkexist.com

William James. www.quotedb.net.

Charles E. Rice. Former CEO of Barnett Bank. www.lexinformatcia.or

Seneca. Roman philosopher, www.ThinkExist.com.

T. S. Eliot (1888–1965). American-born editor, playwright, poet, and critic. www.Thinkexist.com.

Thomas Jefferson (1743–1826). www.quotationspage.com